FIGHTING THE GOOD FIGHT OF FAITH

A Guide to Spiritual Warfare

JOHN MARINELLI

Fighting The Good Fight of Faith
Copyright © 2023 John Marinelli
Ocala, Florida ...All rights reserved.

First Edition: 5/2023

Print ISBN: 978-1-0878-8816-3
eBook ISBN: 978-1-0879-2598-1

Cover and Formatting: Streetlight Graphics
Contact: johnmarinelli@embarqmail.com

TABLE OF CONTENTS

PREFACE

My purpose in writing this book is to call attention to the reality of a real and ever-present danger that faces every human being, especially all, "Born Again," believers in Christ.

Those who are not, "Born Again" will not understand the need to participate in the battle of the ages nor the principles of spiritual warfare. Nevertheless, I speak to anyone who will listen.

My Goal is to educate, clarify, encourage and teach the basics of spiritual self-defense so that the reader can understand and apply Godly principles to everyday situations.

Special attention will be given to the Who; What; When; Where; How; and Why of fighting the good fight of faith. *This is a guide to Spiritual Warfare.*

I will also add some encouraging Christian poetry to the text as a blessing to the reader. Plus, there will be a secret link in the book that will take the reader to a free download of 25 audio files of poems set to music.

I have documented every statement with Bible references so as to show relevance and divine purpose. Most often, the King James version of the Bible is quoted.

INTRODUCTION

When was the last time you got into a fight? Was it a knock down drag our battle or just a few punches? Most of us are gentle and avoid physical contact with the intent to do bodily harm. We just want to be left alone to do our own thing. "Live and let live" is our motto. Anger and violence are not a normal part of our daily routine.

So why all the hoopla about having to fight? What's all this noise about a good fight of faith? I don't hurt anybody and I don't practice evil. Who is it that wants to hurt me? That type of thinking just doesn't make sense.

If that is what you think and the way you feel, good luck in getting through life without going crazy. I heard a sermon the other day where the minister said that 75% of illnesses in America stem from an emotional disorder. Folks are literally going crazy and don't know why.

It is impossible to be neutral in a war that is aimed at your destruction. There is no negotiating with the enemy. Compromise only leads you further down the road to hell and eternal destruction. If you are human, of the Adamic race, you are marked for torment and death by an unseen enemy that God tossed out of his kingdom ages ago.

However, there is hope. Jesus loves you and gave you his Holy Spirit to dwell in you and guide you into all truth so you can live in freedom apart from all seen or unseen enemies.

Evil spirits will not rule over you if you join Jesus in the good fight of faith. Your mindset needs to change from "Me, Myself & I" to focusing on God's will and his teaching on how to fight against your enemies.

We will look at the battle, the enemy, the weapons, the war perspective and other related tools that you can use to keep yourself out of harm's way. This is what I call "Spiritual, Self-Defense."

CHAPTER ONE:

THE FACE OF THE ENEMY

Will our real enemy please stand up? Is it family, business associates, strangers, bad folks, dogmatic religious people or who? The Bible says, "For we wrestle not against flesh and blood, but against principalities, against powers, against the rulers of the darkness of this world, against spiritual wickedness in high places." Ephesians 6:12

We know from reading the Bible that our real enemy is evil and to locate its origin we must realize that it is a matter of morality. We must be able to distinguish between man's morality and God's morality.

God's morality is called Righteousness. Man's morality misses this mark or standard. It can shift and even change with the moods of society. One day it is immoral to have an abortion and the next it is considered a women's health issue that is ok or normal.

We must align ourselves to the morality of God. Why? Because he never changes. He, unlike man, does not waver in character or personality. He is always good, always righteous, always truthful, always right. A good picture is to contrast light with darkness. God is light and there is no darkness in him. He is pure in every way.

Now, let's look at evil. It is anti-God. It does not accept God as the standard for good or should I say righteousness? It projects itself as a replacement for God. It will deceive men and women into thinking that it is good when it is far from being good.

So, what is evil?...It is the rejection of God and all that he stands for.

This attitude is called "SIN" and it is first of all aimed at God; to dishonor him and steal his throne and take control over all of his creation including mankind.

Where did evil begin? According to the Bible, it all began in the heart of Lucifer; an archangel of God that some scholars believe led the worship in heaven. He was magnificent in every way. He led 1/3 of all the angels in a rebellion against God that ended up with all that rebelled being cast out of the heavenly realm. This all happened because Lucifer wanted to be God. Thus, he rebelled and tried to take over as God. This was considered the very first sin and it met with swift judgment.

Here are a few supporting scriptures that reveal the truth.

1. And he, (Jesus), said unto them, (his disciples),"I beheld Satan, as lightning, fall from heaven." Luke 10:18

2. "And there was war in heaven: Michael and his angels fought against the dragon; and the dragon fought and his angels, and prevailed not; neither was their place found any more in heaven. And the great dragon was cast out, that old serpent, called the Devil, and Satan, which deceives the whole world: he was cast out into the earth, and his angels were cast out with him." Revelation 12:7-9

3. "How art thou fallen from heaven, O Lucifer, son of the morning! How art thou cut down to the ground, which didst weaken the nations! For thou hast said in thine heart, I will ascend into heaven, I will exalt my throne above the stars of God: I will sit also upon the mount of the congregation, in the sides of the north: I will ascend above the heights of the clouds; I will be like the Most High. Yet thou shalt be brought down to hell, to the sides of the pit." Isaiah 14:12-15

4. "And the angels which kept not their first estate, but left their own habitation, he hath reserved in everlasting chains under darkness unto the judgment of the great day." Jude v-6

5. "By the multitude of thy merchandise they have filled the midst of thee with violence, and thou hast sinned: therefore, I will cast thee as profane out of the mountain of God: and I will destroy thee, O covering cherub, from the midst of the stones of fire. Thine heart was

lifted up because of thy beauty, thou hast corrupted thy wisdom by reason of thy brightness: I will cast thee to the ground, I will lay thee before kings, that they may behold thee." Ezekiel 28:16-17

By now you probably have noticed different names for evil. They are all the same entity. Evil started in one individual personality, a spiritual being. He sinned against God by trying to be God. Over the centuries that entity has taken on many different names.

There are a lot of folks that do not believe in the existence of a being that is evil. They think that evil comes from the hearts of men and women, boys and girls but not a supernatural being. Jesus spoke at length about this evil being. In fact, the Bible has many different names for him including:

Lucifer, meaning "Morning Star" (Isaiah 14:12)

Ruler of The Demons (Matthew 12:24)

god of This World (2 Corinthians 4:4)

Devil/Accuser (Matthew 4:1)

Prince of the Power of the Air (Ephesians 2:2)

Roaring Lion (1 Peter 5:8)

The Serpent (Genesis 3:1)

Dragon (Revelation 12:9; 20:2)

Adversary (Job 1)

The Tempter (Matthew 4:3)

The anointed Cherub (Ezekiel 28:14)

Beelzebub (Matthew 12:24)

Belial (2 Corinthians 6:15)

Wicked One (Matthew 13:19)

Thief (John 10:10)

Lord of the Flies, the Anti-Christ and Father of Lies are also used to describe this evil being. Jesus referred to him as a thief and said "The thief comes only to steal and kill and destroy; I have come that they may have life, and have it to the full." John 10:10

Peter called him our adversary, the devil. " Be sober, be vigilant; because your adversary the devil, as a roaring lion, walks about, seeking whom he may devour: Whom resist steadfast in the faith, knowing that the same afflictions are accomplished in your brethren that are in the world." I Peter 5:8-9

This evil, being called the devil, first showed up in the Bible in the book of Genesis as the serpent who convinced Eve—who then convinced Adam—to eat forbidden fruit from the "tree of the knowledge." This all happened in the Garden of Eden. As the story goes, after Adam and Eve fell for the devil's conniving ways, they were banished from the Garden of Eden and doomed to a life of mortality.

The devil makes more appearances in the Bible, especially in the New Testament. Jesus and many of his apostles warned people to stay alert for the devil's cunning enticements. It was the devil who tempted Jesus in the wilderness to "fall down and worship him" in exchange for riches and glory. Jesus didn't fall for his deceptive suggestions.

Perhaps the most lasting images of the devil are associated with Hell, which the Bible refers to as a place of everlasting fire prepared for the devil and his angels. Still, the Bible doesn't state that the devil will reign over hell, just that he'll eventually be banished there where he will suffer for all of eternity.

Throughout history, the devil's reputation as an evildoer hasn't changed much. Most Christians still believe he is responsible for much of the world's corruption and chaos.

What's important to realize is that this evil being is a defeated foe. That is evident from what the scriptures say…

Jesus Christ came for two purposes, "to seek and to save that which was lost" (Luke 19:10) and "that he might destroy the works of the devil" (1

John 3:8) "And having spoiled principalities and powers, he made a shew of them openly, triumphing over them in it." (Colossians 2:15)

This is why Peter says we can stand up to that" Roaring Lion", resist him and he will flee from us…because he has no power over us except what we give him. I Peter 5:8

We see the face of evil all around us. The nightly news reveals its character every day. The Bible also tells us about the character of evil as it dwells within the hearts of the human race. Listen to the apostle Paul as he writes to the church of the Galatians.

"This I say then, walk in the Spirit, and ye shall not fulfill the lust of the flesh. For The flesh lusts against the Spirit, and the Spirit against the flesh: and these are contrary the one to the other: so that ye cannot do the things that ye would. But if ye be led of the Spirit, ye are not under the law.

Now the works of the flesh are manifest, which are these; adultery, fornication, uncleanness, lasciviousness, Idolatry, witchcraft, hatred, variance, emulations, wrath, strife, seditions, heresies, envying, murders, drunkenness, rebelling, and such like: of the which I tell you before, as I have also told you in time past, that they which do such things shall not inherit the kingdom of God. (*This is the face of evil and it raises its awful head in many individuals these days.*)

But the fruit of the Spirit is love, joy, peace, longsuffering, gentleness, goodness, faith, meekness, temperance: against such there is no law. And they that are Christ's have crucified the flesh with the affections and lusts.

"If we live in the Spirit, let us also walk in the Spirit. Let us not be desirous of vain glory, provoking one another, envying one another." Gal.5:15-26

Paul contrasts the works of the flesh, which is the character of the fallen man, with the fruit of the Spirit, which is the character of God. Adam was created in the image and likeness of God. He possessed God's very nature, his character, which is Love, Joy, Peace, Longsuffering, Gentleness, Goodness, Faith, Meekness, and Temperance. This is what Adam lost when he disobeyed God. This is what we gain when we are, "Born Again"

Believe it or not, evil is on a mission. Jesus taught us this when he said, "The thief cometh not, but for to steal, and to kill, and to destroy: I am come that they might have life, and that they might have it more abundantly. John 10:10

Jesus contrasted his mission with that of "the thief", which is another title for evil personified. The mission of evil is to Steal, Kill and Destroy. The devil wants to steal your peace, kill your joy and destroy your love so you become like him, evil and full of hate. However, Jesus came that we might have life and that the life we experience be in abundance. His destiny for us is to live not die; to laugh not cry; to love not hate; to be full of goodness not evil. This is what Jesus said he came to seek and to save. That which was lost was the image of God in man.

It's important to know that we were created as the temple of God. Man was to be the throne of God upon the earth. Our hearts were created with the capacity for God to dwell there in perfect harmony.

Satan's mission was to first block God from being seated on his earthly throne, the hearts of men and second to seat himself on that same throne, man's heart, thus ruling the earth and its inhabitance. His power now comes from fallen man whose nature is evil. (Like father/like son) They are both the same.

Evil will not persist forever. It has an end and that end is soon to come. Here's what the Bible says:

1. **Revelation 20:10** "And the devil that deceived them was cast into the lake of fire and brimstone, where the beast and the false prophet are, and shall be tormented day and night for ever and ever." Revelation 20:14-15 "Then Death and Hades were cast into the lake of fire. This is the second death.

2. **Matthew 25:41** "Then he will say to those on his left, 'Depart from me, you accursed, into the eternal fire that has been prepared for the devil and his angels!

3. **Revelation 20:10** And the devil who deceived them was thrown into the

lake of fire and sulfur, where the beast and the false prophet are too, and they will be tormented there day and night forever and ever.

Good will always overcome evil because good is the nature of God and God never loses. At the end of the day, God wins.

Nevertheless, we are in a life and death struggle with the forces evil. Our destiny depends upon how we fight and live our lives here on this earth. The forces of evil can take the unsaved at his or her will because they are children of darkness but the "Born Again" believer is washed in the blood of Christ and has the Holy Spirit of promise inside of him. He or she can overcome. Here are the support scriptures to prove what I am saying.

The Seal of Promise…"Who hath also sealed us, and given the earnest of the Spirit in our hearts." 11 Corinthians 1:22 "In him you also, when you heard the word of truth, the gospel of your salvation, and believed in him, were sealed with the promised Holy Spirit, who is the guarantee of our inheritance until we acquire possession of it, to the praise of his glory." Ephesians 1:13

The Holy Spirit is God's seal on his people, his claim on us as his very own. The Greek word translated "earnest" in these passages is *arrhabōn* which means "a pledge," that is, part of the purchase money or property given in advance as security for the rest. The gift of the Spirit to believers is a down payment on our heavenly inheritance, which Christ has promised us and secured for us at the cross. It is because the Spirit has sealed us that we are assured of our salvation. No one can break the seal of God.

The Greater Spirit… "Ye are of God, little children, and have overcome them: because greater is he that is in you, than he that is in the world." 1 John 4:4 "But ye are not in the flesh, but in the Spirit, if so be that the Spirit of God dwell in you. Now if any man has not the Spirit of Christ, he is none of his." Romans 8:9

The Holy Spirit is inside of us guiding us and leading us along the narrow path to glory. His counsel is greater than any evil spirit that attacks our souls from without. "However, when he, the Spirit of truth, is come, he will guide you into all truth: for he shall not speak of himself; but whatever he shall hear, that shall he speak: and he will show you things to come." John 16:13

The Overcomes... "And they, (The believers), overcame him, (The devil), by the blood of the Lamb, and by the word of their testimony; and they loved not their lives unto the death." Revelation 12:12

The Victory... "Be sober, be vigilant; because your adversary the devil, as a roaring lion, walks about, seeking whom he may devour. Resist him, standing firm in the faith, because you know that the family of believers throughout the world is undergoing the same kind of sufferings." I Peter 5:8-9

So, *the origin of evil* is Lucifer, that wicked angel that rebelled against God and led 1/3 of all the Heavenly Host in a battle against God that ended with all of them being cast out of heaven.

The nature of evil is sin that manifest itself in wickedness, adultery, fornication, uncleanness, lasciviousness, Idolatry, witchcraft, hatred, variance, emulations, wrath, strife, seditions, heresies, Envyings, murders, drunkenness, Revellings, and much more. It is certainly un-holy, un-righteous and immoral. This is the nature of Anti-Christ.

The destiny of evil is total eradication from the face of the earth. The personification of evil in all its forms, whether human or spirit will be placed in the lake of fire for all eternity.

You may be thinking, "If evil is defeated, why are we Christians in a life and death battle with it? The answer is simple...because the devil has no power except that which we give him. He steals it from us with lies and suggestion that appeal to our own evil nature. Multiply this by billions of men, women, boys and girls and you amass lots of power. The devil takes all that power and rules through his captives.

Hear the words of Jesus on this wise...

"When the Son of man shall come in his glory, and all the holy angels with him, then shall he sit upon the throne of his glory: And before him shall be gathered all nations: and he shall separate them one from another, as a shepherd divides *his* sheep from the goats: And he shall set the sheep on his right hand, but the goats on the left. Then the King will say to those on his right, "Come, you who are blessed of my Father, inherit the kingdom prepared for you from the foundation of the world." Then shall he say also unto them on the left hand, "Depart from me, ye cursed, into everlasting fire, prepared for the devil and his angels:" Matthew 25:31-34 & 41

Are you a sheep or are you a goat? Your destiny depends upon your decision. It's time to decide. Being a sheep is to accept Jesus as Lord and Savior and allow him the privilege of sitting on the throne of your life. That involves repenting of your sins, getting off the throne of your life and allowing Jesus his rightful place as your shepherd. Do it today and you'll be "Born Again" into the family of God?

CHAPTER TWO:

WHY DO WE HAVE TO FIGHT?

We do not have to fight. It is not mandatory. You can just float along, living your own lifestyle and doing your own thing. If you believe that, I have a bridge I want to sell you. That type of thinking is all wrong because even the unsaved are subject to evil influences and attacks.

We "Born Again" Christians fight to keep our hearts free from being taken over by Satan. This is the good fight of faith. It is worth doing and it is pleasing to our Heavenly Father.

So, how did man become evil? Wasn't he created in the image of God who is Holy? It all started when Adam and Eve rebelled against God. I do not believe that they were just deceived by the devil and made a mistake. It may have started with deception but in the final analysis, they disobeyed God. *Listen and learn.*

"And the Lord God took the man, and put him into the Garden of Eden to dress it and to keep it. And the Lord God commanded the man, saying, Of every tree of the garden thou may freely eat: But of the tree of the knowledge of good and evil, thou shalt not eat of it: for in the day that thou eat thereof thou shalt surely die." Genesis 2:16-17

As the story goes, they listened to the serpent (devil) who said they would be like God, knowing good and evil when they took the forbidden fruit. The irony of it all is that they were already like God, being made in his very image.

God never wanted man to know evil because it was immoral, unholy and against all that God is. If they experienced evil, they would no longer be in the image of God. They would forfeit their innocence and their character would change from good to evil. There was no in-between or neutrality. Any such rebellion would end in a state of mortality, which would lead to death.

Now see it all happening in real time through the pages of the Bible.

"Wherefore, as by one man, sin entered into the world, and death by sin; and so death passed upon all men, for that all have sinned: (For until the law sin was in the world: but sin is not imputed when there is no law.) Nevertheless, death reigned from Adam to Moses, even over them that had not sinned after the similitude of Adam's transgression, who is the figure of him that was to come." Romans 5:12-14

Death passed upon all men for all have sinned. That is the result of Adam's transgression…He lost the image of God and we were prevented from ever having it. An entire race fell from the grace of God. Instead of being or possessing a character of righteousness we now possess a character that is evil. No longer are we naturally good but rather bent on being our own god and doing our own thing, which is anti-God because it subverts the very plan of God to create man in his own image and likeness.

The nature of evil now exists in humanity. That affects all of society as we, now being our own gods, fight with each other to be the one and only supreme god. That's why Jesus said, "verily, verily, I say unto thee, except a man be born again, he cannot see the kingdom of God." John 3:3

Here's a Biblical example of what Jesus is saying, "And the light shineth in darkness; and the darkness comprehended it not." John 1:5 Darkness just does not understand light. So it is with the natural man. He just does not comprehend the things of God.

We see the face of evil all around us. The nightly news reveals its character every day. The Bible also tells us about the character of evil as it dwells within the hearts of the human race. Listen to the apostle Paul as he writes to the church of the Galatians.

Now the works of the flesh are manifest, which are these; adultery, fornication, uncleanness, lasciviousness, Idolatry, witchcraft, hatred, variance, emulations, wrath, strife, seditions, heresies, envying, murders, drunkenness, rebelling, and such like: of the which I tell you before, as I have also told you in time past, that they which do such things shall not inherit the kingdom of God. (*This is the face of evil and it raises its awful head in many individuals these days.*)

But the fruit of the Spirit is love, joy, peace, longsuffering, gentleness, goodness, faith, meekness, temperance: against such there is no law. And they that are Christ's have crucified the flesh with the affections and lusts.

"If we live in the Spirit, let us also walk in the Spirit. Let us not be desirous of vain glory, provoking one another, envying one another." Gal.5:15-26

Paul contrasts the works of the flesh, which is the character of the fallen man, with the fruit of the Spirit, which is the character of God. Adam was created in the image and likeness of God. He possessed God's very nature, his character, which is Love, Joy, Peace, Longsuffering, Gentleness, Goodness, Faith, Meekness, and Temperance. This is what Adam lost when he disobeyed God. This is what we gain when we are, "Born Again"

Paul also tells us in Galatians, "This I say then, walk in the Spirit, and ye shall not fulfill the lust of the flesh. For The flesh lusts against the Spirit, and the Spirit against the flesh: and these are contrary the one to the other: so that ye cannot do the things that ye would. But if ye be led of the Spirit, ye are not under the law."

The powers of darkness seek total domination of the human race. They will stop at nothing to attain absolute power. Because Jesus defeated them with his death, burial and resurrection as the sacrifice for sin, they call upon the nature of sin now in power within mankind. This sinful nature is what I call, "The Beast Within."

I will attempt to paint a word picture of this beast that lives inside of us all, exposing its character, appetites and plans for the future. I will show its origin and destiny.

I will also reveal God's plan for his children in relationship to living in this world subject to the Beastly appetites that rule most of us today.

"And I stood upon the sand of the sea, and saw a beast rise up out of the sea, having seven heads and ten horns, and upon his horns ten crowns, and upon his heads the name of blasphemy." Revelation 13:1

The apostle John, author of the book of Revelation, tells us about "The Beast" that will rise up out of the sea. Most theologians look at this from a spiritual perspective, not literal. The sea is looked at as the sea of humanity. The seven heads being evil kingdoms that oppose Christ and blaspheme God, and the 10 crowns that exalt the deeds of the flesh as mentioned in Galatians 5:19-20.

" And there was war in heaven: Michael and his angels fought against the dragon; and the dragon fought and his angels, and prevailed not; neither was their place found any more in heaven. And the great dragon was cast out, that old serpent, called the devil, and Satan, which deceived the whole world: he was cast out into the earth, and his angels were cast out with him.

And I heard a loud voice saying in heaven, Now is come salvation, and strength, and the kingdom of our God, and the power of his Christ: for the accuser of our brethren is cast down, which accused them before our God, day and night. And they overcame him by the blood of the Lamb, and by the word of their testimony; and they loved not their lives unto the death.

Therefore rejoice, ye heavens, and ye that dwell in them. Woe to the inhibiters of the earth and of the sea! For the devil is come down unto you, having great wrath, because he knows that he has but a short time." Rev. 7:12 ff

The above verses tell us that there was a war between God and Satan. It took place in Heaven. Notice that Satan is also mentioned by several of his other names, that old serpent, the devil, the accuser of the brethren and the great dragon. We are told that he did not win the battle against the angel Michael and the armies of our God. As a result, he was thrown out of heaven. But God did not allow his enemy to roam the universe. He was cast down to the earth.

Here's what Jude had to say, "I will therefore put you in remembrance, though ye once knew this, how that the Lord, having saved the people out of the land of Egypt, afterward destroyed them that believed not. And the angels which kept not their first estate, but left their own habitation, he hath reserved in everlasting chains under darkness unto the judgment of the great day." Jude 5-6

Jesus said this, "And the seventy returned again with joy, saying, Lord, even the devils are subject unto us through thy name. And he said unto them, I beheld Satan, as lightning, fall from heaven." Luke 10: 17-18

So the war in heaven left God's enemy to be cast to earth where he and all of his angels, now demons, dwell. He knows that his time is short so he makes war on the saints to prevent them from experiencing God's love and blessings. All of this tells me that we are the objects of Satan's wrath.

Peter backs this notion up in his letter I Peter 5:8, "Be sober, be vigilant; because your adversary the devil, as a roaring lion, walks about, seeking whom he may devour:" He says further that we are to resist him steadfast in the Faith and he will flee from us.

Herein is a picture of life on planet earth. We are the objects of the devil's wrath. He roams the earth, not Mars or another galaxy, seeking those who are unaware, unconcerned, and ignorant of the truth. When he finds them, he seeks to steal their peace, kill their dreams and destroy their souls.

So, on the one hand, we have a dragon after us attacking from a distance. But there is another enemy that hides inside of us. He is like the dragon in every way. He is, "The Beast Within."

The Beast was born out of jealousy and pride that led to disobedience. Its image and likeness are the same as the very character of the devil. He wanted to overthrow God and become God. Chapter one gives all the other names that he goes by. As I said before, he found himself on earth, with no power of his own. He had to steal that authority from man who had dominion over every living thing on the earth.

We were to take dominion and rule the planet under the authority and grace of God. But the serpent deceived Eve and talked Adam into disobeying God's command. The result of their actions caused spiritual death to both of them and allowed sin to enter into the hearts of men and pass on through every generation. Romans 5:12 and Genesis 2:15-17.

Romans 5:18-21 tells us, "Therefore as by the offense of one *judgment came* upon all men to condemnation; even so by the righteousness of one *the free gift came* upon all men unto justification of life. For as by one man's disobedience many were made sinners, so by the obedience of one shall many be made righteous. Moreover, the law entered, that the offence might abound. But where sin abounded, grace did much more abound: That as sin hath reigned unto death, even so might grace reign through righteousness unto eternal life by Jesus Christ our Lord."

So, Adam disobeyed God, just like Satan did and, like Satan, was thrown out of God's presence. Man falls from God's glorious presence into the darkness of sin. He lost the image and likeness of God. But God still loved him and made a plan for his restoration. Man would be justified by the blood of Jesus and his righteousness would be imparted to all who believe.

However, the sin that started with Satan filled the void in man's heart when God's Spirit departed. It's important to realize that God breathed into man, the breath of life and that was what made him a living soul. Life is always in relationship to God. If one is dead, he or she has no "breath of life" in them.

Adam possessed the, "Breath of Life," but it was taken away when he disobeyed. How do I know this? Because of Genesis 2:17 that says, "But of the tree of the knowledge of good and evil, thou shalt not eat of it: for in the day that thou eat thereof thou shalt surely die." He died spiritually but ended up as the "Walking Dead" lost in the darkness of sin.

We're all Zombies without the breath of life in us. Just in case you are still a bit confused, the "Breath of Life" is a reference to the Holy Spirit. His infilling is what causes us to be a living soul.

The image and likeness of the beast is exactly the same as Paul describes in Galatians, chapter five, when discussing the works of the flesh. Hear again what he said, "Now the works of the flesh are manifest, which are these; adultery, fornication, uncleanness, lasciviousness, idolatry, witchcraft, hatred, variance, emulations, wrath, strife, seditions, heresies, envying, murders, drunkenness, rebelling, and such like: of the which I tell you before, as I have also told you in time past, that they which do such things shall not inherit the kingdom of God." Galatians 5:19-21

The above list is only a partial list. Paul ends the list with, "and such like" which means there are more but what has already been presented is enough to make his point. All of these attitudes live within us and are what paints the portrait of the "Beast."

We struggle with this evil nature every day. However, we were not the only ones. Hear what Paul said about himself, "For I know that in me (that is, in my flesh,) dwells no good thing: for to will is present with me; but how to perform that which is good I find not. For the good that I would I do not: but the evil which I would not, that I do." Romans 7:18-19 Paul goes on to say that by the grace of God he can find deliverance from the Beast.

This brings up a theological question. Am I a liar because I lie? Or do I lie because I am a liar at heart? Let's see what the scriptures say, "The heart is deceitful above all things, and desperately wicked: who can know it?" Jeremiah 17:9

Jesus said, "Not that which goes into the mouth defiles a man; but that which comes out of the mouth, this defiles a man." Matthew 15:11

The nature of Sin, which entered the human race and passed upon all men, which is the image and likeness of Lucifer or Satan or the devil, whichever you want to call him, defiled mankind. Adam lost the image and likeness of his creator and now has to live with this evil beast inside that drives him to act out all kinds of wickedness in the earth. Just so you know, Image and likeness are other words for character and nature.

We can clearly see the image and likeness of the Beast that lives within us. The work of the flesh is all around us. We are slaves to it and have no way out...or do we?

Paul tells the Galatians in chapter 5, "Stand fast therefore in the liberty wherewith Christ hath made us free, and be not entangled again with the yoke of bondage." "For we, through the Spirit, wait for the hope of righteousness by faith. For in Jesus Christ neither circumcision avails anything, nor uncircumcision; but faith which works by love." "This I say then, walk in the Spirit, and ye shall not fulfill the lust of the flesh. For the flesh lusts against the Spirit, and the Spirit against the flesh: and these are contrary the one to the other: so that ye cannot do the things that ye would. But if ye be led of the Spirit, ye are not under the law." (Not under the law can be looked at as being not under the rule of the flesh or Beast.)

This is good news because it gives us two weapons that we can use to defeat the beast within. The above scripture says..

Wait for the hope of righteousness by Faith.

The hope of righteousness is a *state of mind*, in which we shall enjoy freedom from evil. This poor *body* will no longer suffer from pain but will be healthy, spiritual, powerful, and immortal. The soul will be no more tormented by sin, nor harassed with doubts, and fears — but will be holy, confident, and happy forever. Waiting for it means it is not here yet but is on its way.

This is the righteousness of God, which is by the faith of Jesus Christ, unto all, and upon all, those who believe whether Jew or Gentile.

I say then, seek to realize more of his presence, to feel more of his power, to experience more of his love, and to exhibit more of his fruits in your daily life and conversation. O my soul, see to it that this is your daily experience, and seek grace to say, "I, through the Spirit, wait for the hope of righteousness by faith." James Smith 1860

"This I say then, walk in the Spirit, and ye shall not fulfill the lust of the flesh." Galatians 5:16

The quicker we allow the fruit of God's Spirit to manifest in us, the faster we will move away from the work of the flesh. We cannot hate if we are actively engaging in love. If we allow the peace of God to rule in our hearts, where is there room for anger or thoughts of hostility? If we cultivate the ability to suffer long (Longsuffering) where are critical attitudes and a domineering posture?

If we walk in the Spirit, we cannot walk in the flesh. We are given a free will choice as a Christian to allow the image of God or allow the image of Satan to indwell us and reveal the likeness of the one we serve. We cannot serve them both. We have to reject one in order to serve the other. There is no neutrality.

Ok, I know what you will say next, **"How do I walk in the Spirit?"** *Answer:* 1st. get "Born Again" 2nd. Find out what the fruit of God's Spirit is. 3rd. Do not allow any emotions that are not the fruit to find their way into your thoughts, actions or dreams. The apostle Paul told the Ephesians to," Neither give place to the devil." Ephesians 4:27

Since the devil has placed his image and likeness inside of us and has in effect created a Beast, this scripture fits perfectly. We are told to give those deeds that come from the flesh, no place. To express it in a more dynamic way, we are not to give any place in our hearts and actions to the works of the flesh which are *these*; Adultery, fornication, uncleanness, lasciviousness, Idolatry, witchcraft, hatred, variance, emulations, wrath, strife, seditions, heresies, Envying, murders, drunkenness, revellings, and such like: of the which I tell you before, as I have also told *you* in time past, that they which do such things shall not inherit the kingdom of God. Galatians 5:19-21

We, in effect, put the flesh to death when we give it no place. We take authority over the Beast by walking in the fruit of the Spirit which is, love, joy, peace, longsuffering, gentleness, goodness, faith, Meekness, temperance: against such there is no law. This is accomplished by faith, not our emotional state.

Life in the Spirit is a journey, and while there are many great passages throughout scripture that discuss the role and person of the Holy Spirit, Romans 8 is perhaps one of the best.

These two verses (Rom 8:26-27) are so rich and helpful in our lives in the Spirit.

1. The Spirit is searching our hearts and knows that we have a mind-set that is focused on him, even if we do not know exactly what we are supposed to pray.
2. The result is that our prayers are prayed according to the will of God

because the Holy Spirit is moving us thus to pray and is presenting the prayers that he is guiding us to pray to the Father.

Question? Where does that leave you? As we complete this chapter, have you realized anything? Maybe it's that you are part of a fallen race that has never been translated into the Jesus Generation. Maybe you now realize that you really are spiritually dead and want to be Born Again into the Kingdom of God's dear Son. If this is true, read these scriptures and ask Jesus to come into your heart.

John 3:16 "For God so loved the world, that he gave his only begotten Son, that whosoever believeth in him should not perish, but have everlasting life."

Are you a, **"Whosoever?"**

Romans 3:23 "For all have sinned, and come short of the glory of God;"

All means All, including you and me.

Romans 6:23, "For the wages of sin is death; but the gift of God is eternal life through Jesus Christ our Lord."

Death is inevitable but God has a gift for everyone who accepts Jesus. That gift is eternal life.

"I tell you, Nay: but, except [unless] ye repent, ye shall all likewise perish" **(Luke 13:3,5).**

"But now [God] commandeth [commands] all men everywhere to repent" **(Acts 17:30).**

The final decision is up to you. You can repent, turn from your wicked ways or those ways that are of the flesh and receive Jesus as your savior. He so loved you that he went to the cross as your substitute. He so loved you that he lived a life without sin so he could be the captain of your salvation. He is calling for you to come to him by faith in his finished work of grace.

Why Do We have To Fight? We fight because the devil attacks us from every side and the beast attacks us from within. If we don't fight, we will fall under the domination and control of Satan. That may be ok for some folks but not for me and hopefully not for you.

We are children of God and joint-heirs with Christ. We are ambassadors of Christ in the earth and we will lay down our lives unto the death if necessary to follow Jesus and honor God, the Father. We do not want to be included with the "Walking Dead" that will experience the wrath of God that will fall upon the wicked.

CHAPTER THREE:

WHERE IS THE BATTLEFIELD?

The Battle is everywhere. It can be in the workplace, in the home, in church, everywhere you live and go. However, the battlefield is in your mind. The devil has a tool box full of tricks, snares and lies. They are all fashioned towards your emotions and temperament.

Most folks are unaware of the "Wiles" of the devil. In fact, over 40% of Americans do not even believe that there is a real devil, only that he is a symbol for evil. (Pew Report)

The Bible tells us about his tricks. His purpose is to snare us with one or more of his tools thereby creating a, "Stronghold" in our lives, from which he can rule over us.

The literal meaning of a "Stronghold" is a fortified armed encampment that can be protected.

A "Snare" is a device or trap that is used to capture a prey. It can be a hunter's trap for small game or a net that is used to catch fish in the sea.

The purpose of tricks, snares, and other tools in "The Devil's Toolbox" is to capture you, and dominate your thoughts and actions with the ultimate goal of manifesting his evil character through you. Hear what Jesus said about the thief, as he referred to the devil.

" The thief cometh not, but for to steal, and to kill, and to destroy: I am come that they might have life, and that they might have it more abundantly." John 10:10

Whatever you call this, "Evil Being" you have to know, without a shadow of a doubt, that he is real and he is after you to steal your dreams, kill any hope of happiness and destroy everything that is good in your life. He wants you dead but not before he torments you for a lifetime.

!!! News Flash !!!

The good news is that Jesus has defeated the devil and he has no power over you but what you give him. That's right, he has to get you to use your own "Free Will" to accept his lie. That's how he takes control. Let's see what the scriptures say so you know that I am not making this up.

"And having spoiled principalities and powers, he (Jesus) made a shew of them openly, triumphing over them in it." Colossians 2:5

Jesus spoiled all evil principalities and powers. That is a total defeat. Then he made an open shew…this denotes an old Roman picture of conquest over enemies. The evil king and leaders were tied by a rope to the back of a chariot and led down the middle of the city streets in a procession of conquest so everyone could see and laugh at the defeated foe. This is total victory.

Adam & Eve were not forced to submit to the devil when he was tempting them in the Garden of Eden. They had to engage their free will to do what the devil suggested.

There's Always A Choice

The devil's power comes from your fleshly appetites. He has no power of his own. He must tap into your sinful nature and use it to accomplish his will. If you give him no place, he cannot do anything. He remains powerless.

We have already seen one tool that is in the devil's toolbox. It is, "The Lie" Jesus, speaking to some religious leaders of his day, said this…

"Ye are of your father the devil, and the lusts of your father ye will do. He was a murderer from the beginning, and abode not in the truth, because there is no truth in him. When he speaks a lie, he speaks of his own: for he is a liar, and the father of it." John 8"44

Lies That Kill, Steal & Destroy

How many times have we believed a lie? The politicians promise all kinds of things but never deliver. Are they lying? We believe their lies and then what?

Here are a few lies that the devil uses to cause us to do what he wants.

1. Drugs can't really hurt you. Try some and see for yourself.
2. Smoking is not really addictive.
3. Sex before marriage doesn't really hurt anyone.
4. Lying is ok as long as no one is hurt.
5. Taking a pen from work is not really stealing.
6. Drinking alcohol is ok. It's cool.

Now let's look at some other lies that are active in modern society.

Ideology That Contradicts Bible Truth

The way you think is the basis for how you act and the way you live your life. There are certain lies that seek to alter your thought processes thereby changing your viewpoint. Here are a few:

There Is Only One True Church.

All the others are false. You must belong to our church in order to be saved. We are the true church of God.

This ideology is so untrue. Salvation does not come as a result of a church membership. Nor does it come from a, "True Religion." It comes from the finished work of Jesus Christ on the cross. He paid the price of sin with his own blood. Hear what the scriptures say...

"Much more then, having now been justified by his blood, we shall be saved from the wrath of God through him. For if while we were enemies we were reconciled to God through the death of his Son, much more, having been reconciled, we shall be saved by his life. And not only this, but we also exult in God through our Lord Jesus Christ, through whom we have now received the reconciliation." Romans 5:9-11

You Don't Have To Believe In Jesus To Attain Eternal Life.

The truth is, you do have to believe in Jesus to be saved and will not see heaven unless you accept him as Savior and Lord. Hear what was said to the people of Israel.

"Be it known unto you all, and to all the people of Israel, that by the name of Jesus Christ of Nazareth, whom ye crucified, whom God raised from the dead, even by him doth this man stand here before you whole. This is the stone, which was set at naught of you builders, which is become the head of the corner. Neither is there salvation in any other: for there is none other name under heaven given among men, whereby we must be saved." Acts 4:10-12

We Are All Children of God

Listen again to the scriptures. They reveal the truth.

"For as many as are led by the Spirit of God, they are the sons of God. For ye have not received the spirit of bondage again to fear; but ye have received the Spirit of adoption, whereby we cry, Abba, Father.

If I Try To Be Good, That's Enough, Right? The Spirit itself bears witness with our spirit, that we are the children of God:" Romans 8:14

The Bible tells us that even religious leaders will not see God's kingdom unless they are, "Born Again" We must be, "Born Again" in order to see God's kingdom. That's what Jesus said. Keep reading!

"There was a man of the Pharisees, named Nicodemus, a ruler of the Jews: The same came to Jesus by night, and said unto him, Rabbi, we know that thou art a teacher come from God: for no man can do these miracles that thou doest, except God be with him. Jesus answered and said unto him, Verily, verily, I say unto thee, except a man be born again, he cannot see the kingdom of God." John 3:3

There Are Many Ways To Heaven.

The lie is that we're all climbing the same mountain but by different paths.

In other words, there are many ways to attain eternal life. This is in direct contrast to what Jesus said. Listen...

"Enter ye in at the strait gate: for wide is the gate, and broad is the way, that leads to destruction, and many there be which go in thereat:" Matthew 7:13

The narrow gate is Jesus. He said himself that...well, read it for yourself...

"Let not your heart be troubled: ye believe in God, believe also in me. In my Father's house are many mansions: if it were not so, I would have told you. I go to prepare a place for you. And if I go and prepare a place for you, I will come again, and receive you unto myself; that where I am, there ye may be also. And whither I go ye know, and the way ye know. Thomas saith unto him, Lord, we know not whither thou goest; and how can we know the way? Jesus saith unto him, I am the way, the truth, and the life: no man cometh unto the Father, but by me." John 14:6

False Religions That Teach Heresy

How often have you heard someone say. "It doesn't matter what religion you follow. You'll still end up in heaven." This lie extends to multi culturalism as well. People say it doesn't matter if you are Hindu, Muslim, Jew, Buddhist, Catholic–whatever. It's not a religion that saves us but rather a relationship with Jesus Christ.

There are many false religions in this world. I call some of them, "Isms." They teach heresy and lead people astray. They distort the truth, deny the deity of Christ and create a bondage that is very hard to break. Here are a few "Isms" to stay clear of. These are Anti-Christ.

Relativism – Relativism is the idea that there is no such thing as truth. The devil doesn't want you to believe in truth because if there is not truth, then there is also no right and wrong, and if there is no right and wrong, then anything goes. He can tempt you into sin much more easily if he can first get you to believe there is no such thing as sin. Relativism is everywhere in our society. It takes many different forms.

Under Relativism I can do my own thing. I can ignore any truth that does not line up with what I think. I am right all the time because there is no right or wrong, just whatever I want. This makes me my own god. How sad!

Utilitarianism – In Short…universalism is a theological doctrine that all human beings will eventually be saved: the principles and practices of a liberal Christian denomination founded in the 18th century originally to uphold the belief in "universal" salvation is now united with Unitarianism.

Here is the melting pot of all kinds of beliefs. You can believe anything you want and still be a member of this church because there is no standard or rule of practice, only what you think is right. The problem is…what we think is right is often wrong and with the devil lying to us; we can be easily misled unless we know God's truth. Jesus said…

"Take heed therefore that the light which is in thee be not darkness." Luke 11:35

Jesus knew that much of what was being presented as truth or light was not truth at all. It was actually darkness. We need to stay away from such as this.

Atheism - Atheism is defined as the disbelief or lack of belief in the existence of God. Whereas, Theism is the belief in the existence of a God, especially belief in one God as creator of the universe, intervening in it and sustaining a personal relation to his creatures.

This non-religion premise has in modern times become a religion unto itself. It denies God any place in reality and sets man up as his own god. The end of this can only be eternal death.

"There is a way which seems right unto a man, but the end thereof are the ways of death." Proverbs 14:12

Mormonism - The Mormon religion, (Mormonism), whose followers are known as Mormons and Latter Day Saints (LDS), was founded less than two hundred years ago by a man named Joseph Smith. He claimed to have received a personal visit from God the Father and Jesus Christ who told him that all churches and their creeds were an abomination. Joseph Smith then set out to begin a brand-new religion that claims to be the "only true church on earth.

This doctrine is a lie and a distortion of the truth. It is a humanistic approach to religion that denies the deity of Christ, The God Head, The Gifts of The Spirit and many other Bible norms.

Socialism - By the late 19th century, socialism emerged as "the most influential secular movement of the twentieth century, worldwide. It is a political ideology (or world view), a wide and divided political movement" Socialist parties and ideas remain a political force with varying degrees of power and influence on all continents. They head up national governments in many countries around the world.

Today, some socialists have also adopted the causes of other social movements, such as environmentalism, feminism and progressivism. They reject religion, faith and are anti-God·

Satanism - is a group of ideological and philosophical beliefs based on Satan. Contemporary religious practice of Satanism began with the founding of the Church of Satan in 1966, although a few historical precedents exist.

Prior to the public practice, Satanism existed primarily as an accusation by various Christian groups toward perceived ideological opponents, rather than a self-identity. Satanism, and the concept of Satan, has also been used by artists and entertainers for symbolic expression.

Liberalism - Unlike traditional liberalism, there is a certain element of tyranny within the modern liberal movement. In past centuries, liberalism was used to literally liberate people from the rule of kings and tyrants.

Modern liberalism is now imposing its immoral beliefs on society. It is a forced movement that is functioning more like a tyranny than any other liberal beliefs have ever done. The premise of liberalism is mainly centered in anti-conservativism which rejects moral laws and respect for tradition.

The devil pushes liberalism more on the young, encouraging immoral behavior or anything that is anti-God.

Legalism... (or nomism), in Messianic/Christian theology, is the act of putting the Law of Moses above the gospel, which is 1 Corinthians 15:1-4, by establishing requirements for salvation beyond faith (trust) in Jesus Christ, specifically, trust in His finished work - the shedding of his blood for our sins, and reducing the broad, inclusive, and general precepts of the Bible to narrow and rigid moral codes.

It is an over-emphasis of discipline of conduct, or legal ideas, usually implying an allegation of misguided rigor, pride, superficiality, the neglect of mercy, and ignorance of the grace of God or emphasizing the letter of law at the expense of the spirit.

Here are a few non "isms" but equally anti-God:

Witchcraft – This is the practice of magic or sorcery by anyone outside the religious mainstream of a society. This term is used in different ways in different times and places. Witchcraft is part of the Occult that deny God and rejects Jesus as Lord. It is centered in mysticism and preys on uniformed folks that seek spiritual answers.

Jehovah's Witness - The Jehovah's Witnesses are best known for going door-to-door. You have probably seen them in your area, and more than likely they have knocked on your door. They recently spent over 1.2 billion hours in one year proclaiming the so-called "good news of Jehovah and His Kingdom".

Jehovah's Witnesses reject the Trinity, believing Jesus to be a created being and the Holy Spirit to essentially be the inanimate power of God. Jehovah's Witnesses reject the concept of Christ's substitutionary atonement and instead hold to a ransom theory, that Jesus' death was a ransom payment for Adam's sin.

New Age - The **New Age** is a term applied to a range of spiritual or religious beliefs and practices that developed in Western nations during the 1970s. Precise scholarly definitions of the movement differ in their emphasis, largely as a result of its highly eclectic structure. Although analytically often considered to be religious, those involved in it typically prefer the designation of "spiritual" and rarely use the term "New Age" themselves.

Many scholars of the subject refer to it as the **New Age movement**. It is very close to Universalism in that it believes in the spiritual but denied the truth of One God, One Lord and One Spirit, which is the centerpiece of Christianity.

Islam - "The source of the word, (Allah), who is the Islamic god, goes back to pre-Muslim times. Islam calls Allah god, which is not the God of the bible. Allah has about 1.6 billion followers worldwide. In 2010, Muslims made up 23.2% of the global population. According to the Encyclopedia of Religion, Allah corresponded to the Babylonian god Baal, and Arabs knew of him long before Mohammed worshipped him as the supreme god.

Before Islam, the Arabs recognized many gods and goddesses; each tribe had their own deity. There were also nature deities. Allah was the god of the local Quarish tribe, which was Mohammed's tribe before he invented Islam to lead his people out of their polytheism. Allah was then known as the Moon god, who had three daughters who were viewed as intercessors for the people.

Demonic Suggestions

We could go on and on but you get the point, right? There is a suggestion made by the devil that is a lie. It is presented as truth. If we believe it, we fall prey to the devil's manipulation and eventual take over. He wants to be the, "Voice In Your Head" that lord's over you. He wants to lead you away from all that is Godly. He wants to sit on God's throne which is in your heart.

All that has been mentioned above deal with lies that if accepted and believed will capture you and lead you from the light of God's glory into darkness.

Pitfalls In Personality...The Deeds of The Flesh

Now here are a few inward traps that cause sickness in our bodies and hasten our demise. These character flaws are used by the devil to capture us and take us down the broad road to destruction. They are a product of our own fallen nature. The Bible calls them the "Works of The Flesh." There is a full list in Galatians chapter five. I present them again because it is important that you know them and recognize them in you when they raise their evil heads.

"Now the works of the flesh are manifest, which are these; adultery, fornication, uncleanness, lasciviousness, Idolatry, witchcraft, hatred, variance, emulations, wrath, strife, seditions, heresies, envying, murders, drunkenness, revellings, and such like: of the which I tell you before, as I have also told you in time past, that they which do such things shall not inherit the kingdom of God." Galatians 5:19-21

All the devil has to do is to suggest a plan of action that involves one or more of these character flaws and if you buy it, you're off into the flesh that cannot please God. If he tells you that your brother's wife is sexy and you probably could have her and you start thinking of the reality of that encounter, you have committed adultery. Lust takes over and ego soars and imaginations rule. You don't have to do the act, just think about it.

The same is true of pornography. If you are just looking, it's still fornication in your mind and that will distort your sense of morality and steal your Godly values.

"But I say unto you, that whosoever looks on a woman to lust after her hath committed adultery with her already in his heart." Matthew 5:28

The devil doesn't make you do anything. He only suggests it and sometimes it can be a powerful illusion like he did with Jesus in the wilderness. It is your own will that takes you down the road to hell or resist him and go on in the Spirit.

The Bible says that Satan, (the devil) is the accuser of the brethren. Here is the exact scripture…

"And I heard a loud voice saying in heaven, Now is come salvation, and strength, and the kingdom of our God, and the power of his Christ: for the accuser of our brethren is cast down, which accused them before our God, day and night. And they overcame him by the blood of the Lamb, and by the word of their testimony; and they loved not their lives unto the death." Revelation 12:10-11

The, "They" in Verse 11 is us, The Brethren. We can and do overcome this accuser with The Blood of The Lamb, The Word of Our Testimony and Because We Loved Not Our Lives Unto Death. See?...we can have victory.

You may be wondering what types of accusations are made against us. Here are a few:

1. You are ugly and stupid.
2. You are not worthy of anyone's love.
3. You cannot be saved because you have done too many bad things.
4. You are a bad person so go ahead and be bad.
5. And so on

Demonic accusations are meant to cause doubt, fear, low self-esteem and worry among other things. However, the scripture (Revelation 12:11) also says that the accusation is against you before the throne of God. He accuses you in front of all the host of heaven. All the things you do wrong are brought before the court of God's Justice. He is constantly telling God how bad you are. If we are "Born Again" Jesus, who is seated at the right hand of God, The Father, is interceding on our behalf, saying in effect, "He or she is mine. Their names are written in the Lamb's Book of Life. They've been washed in my Blood."

Watch Out For These

Temptation... Satan nags us to act on addictive urges and to entertain selfishness and greed. How can we resist this direct temptation? Jesus used a two-step defensive technique: first, he ordered Satan to leave; then he quoted scripture. You have the right to tell Satan to leave when you are confronted with temptation. There is great power in memorizing scripture, as Jesus did. Scripture power not only intimidates Satan, but it also brings the Spirit of God into your heart. Listen again to the scriptures...

"There hath no temptation taken you but such as is common to man: but God is faithful, who will not suffer you to be tempted above that ye are able; but will with the temptation also make a way to escape, that ye may be able to bear it". I Corinthians 10:

Deception… The devil has been called "the great deceiver." He attempts to counterfeit every true principle the Lord presents. Although Satan will lie to you, you can count on the Spirit of God to tell you the truth. That's why the gift of the Holy Ghost is so essential.

Contention… Satan is the father of contention. He delights in seeing good people argue. When there is contention in your home or workplace, immediately stop whatever you are doing and seek to make peace. It doesn't matter who started it.

"Be not hasty in thy spirit to be angry: for anger rests in the bosom of fools." Ecclesiastes 7:9

We do not want to be counted with the fools of this world. However, the devil wants us there so he and the rest of the inhabitants of planet earth can laugh at us.

Discouragement… Satan effectively uses this tool on the most faithful Saints when all else fails. President Ezra Taft Benson (1899–1994) gave suggestions for fighting discouragement. They include serving others; working hard and avoiding idleness; practicing good health habits; seeking a priesthood blessing; listening to inspiring music; counting your blessings; and setting goals and above all, as the scriptures teach, we are to pray always.

When we get discouraged, it is usually because we didn't get our way. Something hindered us from being on top. Instead, we got fired, lost in a card game, watched as our spouse left us, or some other bad thing.

There is an easy remedy for discouragement. That is to make Jesus the Lord of your life and trust him in every circumstance. This takes the burden of responsibility off of you and allows God to work out everything for good. (See Romans 8:28)

Situational Ethics That Replace Absolute Truth

This is another name for moral relativism. The idea is that nothing is right or wrong except for the intentions and circumstances of the moral choice. If you mean well and the circumstances justify it, then what you've chosen to do is okay. Huge numbers of Christians have accepted this premise to justify abortion. If it feels right, it must be ok. However, feeling right is not the same as God's Moral Laws. His Word is absolute, no matter what you or I feel.

The devil will always invoke a situational ethic into the mix so as to divert our thinking away from the absolute truth of God's Word. Here's an example of situational sin...

Scientific Facts That Contradict Biblical Revelation

This is the idea that the only kind of truth is scientific truth. It's a powerful lie of Satan because it is one of those things, which is simply assumed in society.

"We all know that science has disproved the Bible, right?" Wrong. All truth is God's truth and true science is always the sister of true theology. Scientism is an offshoot of atheism. "There is no God. There are just the laws of science. That's all." No! No! No! That's wrong.

This Godless doctrine ushered in evolution back in the 18th century. It was the devil's way of offering a believable platform for those who did not want to follow God. As you may know, this theory says we evolved over millions of years into what we are today, with no divine influences. Thus, we are our own gods and masters of our own destinies. Hitler used this theory to kill six million Jews in WWII. African Americans were once considered substandard beings because of this theory. Hear what the Bible says...

"And as it is appointed unto men once to die, but after this the judgment: So Christ was once offered to bear the sins of many; and unto them that look for him shall he appear the second time without sin unto salvation. " Hebrews 9:27-28 We should be looking to Jesus, not science.

False Prophets & Teachers

Here's what the Bible says about false prophets and teachers...

"And many false prophets shall rise, and shall deceive many." Matthew 24:11 Mark 13:22 says it this way..."For false Christs and false prophets shall rise, and shall shew signs and wonders, to seduce, if it were possible, even the elect."

It is clear that the goal of these false prophets is to deceive. Their teachings are false. Their efforts are for self-empowerment. Their doctrines are demonic in nature. Have you ever heard of Rev. Jones that took his congregation overseas and killed them all... but only after abusing the females and stealing their wealth?

Let's bring this on the level of the average Christian who can also be a false teacher. Here again what Jesus said to His disciples...

"For many shall come in my name, saying, I am Christ; and shall deceive many.: Matthew 24:5

The term, "Christ" literally means Anointed. What is really being said is that there will be many that claim to be anointed of God, like Jesus was anointed. This is the mark of a Christian but these false Christians are not anointed. They just claim to be. They will be able to talk the talk but do not follow the truth of the gospel message. A good example is the Mormon Church. These days they claim to be the Latter-Day Saints and call themselves Christians. However, they believe very differently. Their doctrines are anti-Christ. These false believers are sprinkled throughout all main line denominations.

How many folks do you know that profess to be a Christian but have no knowledge of what it really means? Some even claim to be anointed when they operate in the flesh and promote a secular gospel that is akin to Humanism.

Sickness & Disease

The devil will use sickness and disease to steal our strength, destroy our health and kill our healthy cells. However, we are challenged to believe another report. This time it's not the doctor's diagnosis but the Word of God.

The question is, **"Does God Want You To Be Healed"** or **Will He Say No To Your Plea?** I was a Baptist, way back when. Our prayer for healing always started with, **"If It Be Thy Will"** We never knew if it was God's will to heal or not. Maybe there was a reason why he didn't want us to be healed. Then I looked into the scriptures and found these declarations:

Healed By His Stripes

- "He is despised and rejected of men; a man of sorrows, and acquainted with grief: and we hid as it were our faces from him; he was despised, and we esteemed him not. Surely, he hath borne our griefs, and carried our sorrows: yet we did esteem him stricken, smitten of God, and afflicted. But he was wounded for our transgressions, he was bruised for our iniquities: the chastisement of our peace was upon him; and with his stripes we are healed." Isaiah 5.:3-6 "Who hath believed our report? and to whom is the arm of the Lord revealed?" Isaiah 53:1

Note: This suffering servant, spoken of by Isaiah, has borne our grief and carried our sorrows. He was stricken of God. He was wounded for our transgressions and bruised for our iniquities. The chastisement of our peace was upon him….and With His Stripes We Are Healed.

The only person that qualifies in all these areas is Jesus. Isaiah clearly said that our healing is in His stripes, which were the beatings and bruises and wounds. His blood and subsequent death brought healing to those who believed his report.

Healed By The Prayer of Faith

"Is anyone among you sick? Let them call the elders of the church to pray over them and anoint them with oil in the name of the Lord. And the prayer offered in faith will make the sick person well; the Lord will raise them up. If they have sinned, they will be forgiven." James 5:14-15

Healed Through Worship

"Worship the LORD your God, and his blessing will be on your food and water. I will take away sickness from among you…" Exodus 23:25

Healed By The Lord, Just Because

"But I will restore you to health and heal your wounds,' declares the LORD" Jeremiah 30:17

"I have seen their ways, but I will heal them; I will guide them and restore comfort to Israel's mourners, creating praise on their lips. Peace to those far and near," says the LORD. "And I will heal them." Isaiah 57:18-19

Healing By God's Divine Will

"He himself bore our sins" in his body on the cross, so that we might die to sins and live for righteousness; "by his stripes (wounds) you were healed." 1 Peter 2:24

"He gives strength to the weary and increases the power of the weak." Isaiah 40:29

"Then they cried to the LORD in their trouble, and he saved them from their distress. He sent out his word and healed them; he rescued them from the grave. Let them give thanks to the LORD for his unfailing love and his wonderful deeds for mankind." Psalms 107:19-21

"He heals the brokenhearted and binds up their wounds." Psalms 147:3

"Jesus went through all the towns and villages, teaching in their synagogues, proclaiming the good news of the kingdom and healing every disease and sickness." Matthew 9:35

The Devil Uses Sickness & Diseases To Oppress The Children of God

The Bible tells us "How God anointed Jesus of Nazareth with the Holy Ghost and with power: who went about doing good, and healing all that were oppressed of the devil; for God was with him.".

"And when they came to the crowd, a man came up to him and, kneeling before him, said, "Lord, have mercy on my son, for he has seizures and he suffers terribly. For often he falls into the fire, and often into the water. And I brought him to your disciples, and they could not heal him." And Jesus answered, "O faithless and twisted generation, how long am I to be with you? How long am I to bear with you? Bring him here to me." And Jesus rebuked the demon and it came out of him, and the boy was healed instantly" Matthew 17:14-18

Is there any question as to God not wanting his children to be healed? There wasn't a time when someone did not get healed. Sometimes it was because they asked to be healed. Other times God just healed them.

We should never say, "If It Be Thy Will." Based upon these scriptures, we should now know that it is and always will be God's will that we be healed.

Why Then, In Our Day, Do Many Sick Folk Not Get Healed?

That is a good question. I have prayed for some and seen them receive their healing. I have also prayed and saw nothing happen. Here's what I have surmised after more than 60 years of following Christ.

Some folks just do not believe that Jesus can or will heal them. Some have more faith in doctors and pills than they do in Jesus. Some secretly like their condition because they get sympathy and attention that they would ordinarily not get if they were well. Some get disability checks and do not have to work and like it that way. Some are reaping what they sowed and have to endure it. Some are weak in faith and lose hope before they are healed. I remember the words of Jesus. He said, "Be it unto you according to your faith." Matthew 9:29

Still others just do not get healed and do not know why. They pray, they cry, they plead and nothing happens. The woman with the issue of blood was bound for 18 years. The blind man was blind from birth so God's power could be used to glorify the name of Jesus. Sometimes there are reasons why things don't go, as we so desire.

This one thing I do know…It is God's will that all of us be in good health and prosper. Until he tells me otherwise, I will continue to seek him for my healing and believe that I have what I ask for. In fact, I regularly call forth healing into existence. It is an unseen reality that is and is not but will soon be.

Sickness can come upon us from several sources. If we smoke and get lung cancer, it is our fault, not the devil's or even God's. If we drink alcohol in excess and become an alcoholic, whose fault, is it? If we work ourselves to death and come down with a cold or get sick, is it anyone's fault other than our own?

In a world tainted by sin, sickness and disease will always be with us, at least until Jesus comes again. We are fallen beings, with physical bodies prone to disease and illness. Some sickness is simply a result of the natural course of things in this world. Sickness can also be the result of a demonic attack. However, sickness does not originate with God.

The Bible, again says, "The Lord is not slack concerning his promise, as some men count slackness; but is longsuffering to us-ward, **not willing that any should perish,** but that all should come to repentance." 2 Peter 3:9

If God does not want us to perish, that is a clear indication that he does not afflict us with a sickness or a disease that would cause our demise. It's just not logical.

I believe I have made a good case against, "If It Be Thy Will". All these scriptures lead me to one big conclusion…It is God's will that we be healed and stay in good health.

Expectations That Discourage "Free Will" Choices

The devil often uses people to do his bidding. It could be a parent, co-worker, teacher or even a friend. Their efforts to impose expectation on you can be very painful. It could be an immoral act, a restrictive influence or even a command that goes against what you feel is right.

This type of expectation puts pressure on you to be or do what they want instead of what you feel is right. It is a form of oppression.

On the other hand, God's expectations are designed to give you the greatest freedom and blessings possible. Hear what the psalmist said many years ago, "My soul, wait thou only upon God; for my expectation is from him." Psalm 62:5

If you feel that what others are expecting of you is not in God's plan for your life or that you just do not have peace about what is expected of you, reject it, no matter who it is. Your peace is more important than their expectations. That will keep the devil at bay and you free. We should always look for what God would expect of us and reject the expectations of others. By the way, God's expectations are clearly revealed in the Bible.

Illusions & Mind Games That Confuse And Manipulate

The devil will also use illusions to confuse you or cause you to think that he has power over you or cause you to think that he owns the world and even the people in it. Listen to how he tried to trick Jesus…

"The devil said to him, (Jesus), "I will give you all the power and glory of these kingdoms. All of it has been given to me, and I give it to anyone I please." Luke 4:6

The devil did not own the kingdoms of the world. Nor did he have the power and glory of those kingdoms. They belong to God. "The earth is the Lord's, and the fullness thereof; the world, and they that dwell therein. For he hath founded it upon the seas, and established it upon the floods." Psalm 24:1-2

As the story goes, the devil took Jesus up to the pinnacle of the temple to show him all the kingdoms of the world. The problem is, you cannot see all the kingdoms of the world from that vantage point.

The devil likes to play with your mind and manipulate your imagination. He will play mind games with you in hopes that you will engage your imagination to mentally see what is being suggested. It all takes place in the mind and it is usually a bold-faced lie.

Here's how it works with folks today. A thought enters the mind from the devil or one of his demons. The thought is an image of a kid in a store looking at a toy truck. The suggestion is, "Take it, no one is looking. The kid mentally sees himself playing with it and sees all his friends being envious of him because he has the new truck and they do not… so he steals it. The kid is you and your feelings are fully engaged.

It could be a lonely guy wishing he could find a girl. Suddenly a thought enters his mind. It's of an old girlfriend. Another thought tells him, "Boy I could really …you can fill in the rest. Now he is mentally engaged in a sexual act that is not real…thus, he falls into sin, gets depressed because he realizes he is still alone, hates himself for thinking that way and becomes suicidal.

The devil will always suggest that you picture things that you don't or cannot have. He does this because it is tormenting and he loves to torment us as he takes us down the road to hell. His ultimate goal is to drive you to a place where you will act out your fantasies. Thus, comes rape, murder, watching pornography and all the deeds of the flesh listed in Galatians chapter five.

The thing to realize is…not all of our thoughts are ours. We get some from the devil, from our own sinful nature and even some from the Holy Spirit. We have to try the spirits to be sure they are from God before we act on them. Hear what the apostle John says…

"Beloved, believe not every spirit, but try the spirits whether they are of God: because many false prophets are gone out into the world. Hereby know ye the Spirit of God: Every spirit that confesses that Jesus Christ is come in the flesh is of God: And every spirit that confesses not that Jesus Christ is come in the flesh is not of God: and this is that spirit of antichrist, whereof ye have heard that it should come; and even now already is it in the world." I John 4:1-5

Jesus used the scriptures to defeat the devil. He said, **"IT IS WRITTEN."** He knew the Word of God and used it to put down the lie and dispel the illusion. This means if we want to defeat the devil, we also need to know what is written so we can use it at the appropriate time. I am referring to the written Word of God, the Bible. If we are tempted to steal, we can say, it is written, "Thou Shalt Not Steal" Exodus 20:15 This will dispel the illusion. Then we can tell the devil to take a hike.

Knowing scripture is essential to winning the battle. Here's what Paul said to the Corinthian church back in the first century, "For the weapons of our warfare are not carnal but mighty in God for pulling down strongholds, casting down imaginations and every high thing that exalts itself above the knowledge of God, bringing every thought into captivity to the obedience of Christ" II Corinthians 10:4-5

If we know the scripture, we can cast down every imagination that is against the knowledge of God. That is what Jesus did. He knew that God said that man was not to steal and he used that truth to overcome the devil.

Remember, what God did in the Old Testament was then. We are now in a New Covenant where God's grace (Unmerited Favor) rules the day. God does not punish his children with disease or sickness. His loving hand is extended towards all who believe. He wants them all to come to repentance.

I am sure you will find other tools that should be added to the devil's tool-box. I have shown you enough to open your eyes to the, "Wiles" of the devil in hopes that you search out ways to defend yourself. We are in a fight for our lives that has eternal consequences.

The apostle Peter gave us a clear and present danger with an assurance of victory. Here's what he said, "Be sober, be vigilant; because your adversary the devil, as a roaring lion, walks about, seeking whom he may devour: Whom resist steadfast in the faith, knowing that the same afflictions are accomplished in your brethren that are in the world." I Peter 5:8-9

The apostle John leaves us with this…"And now, little children, abide in him; that, when he shall appear, we may have confidence, and not be ashamed before him at his coming." I John 2:28

I have sought to expose the "Wiles" of the devil and the various tools in his tool box so you can see what you are up against. If you are not aware, you will be pulled into darkness and captured by the evil forces that lurk in the night.

I have showed you Biblical examples of evil as well as its rule in the earth through false religions, doctrines and teachings so you can avoid them.

I have showed you the battlefield and how Satan attacks from everywhere around you and even through the Beast that hides within your human nature so you can learn how to resist and stay free.

Now, let's look at some weapons we can use to defeat the forces of evil. Remember, these evil forces have already been subdued by Jesus. They are defeated and are now forced to steal your birthright to have any authority. If you stand firm in the Lord, the enemy cannot hurt you.

Remember what Peter, the apostle said, "Be sober, be vigilant; because your adversary the devil, as a roaring lion, walketh about, seeking whom he may devour: Whom resist steadfast in the faith, knowing that the same afflictions are accomplished in your brethren that are in the world." I Peter 5:8-9

CHAPTER FOUR:

WHAT WEAPONS DO WE USE?

We are not helpless in this good fight of faith. God has given us weapons to use in self-defense of our being and our family. However, these weapons are not tanks, machineguns, bombs or other carnal things. They are spiritual. Remember, we fight against spiritual wickedness in high places and the rulers of darkness…not flesh and blood. Ephesians 6:12

"For the weapons of our warfare are not carnal, but mighty through God to the pulling down of strong holds; Casting down imaginations, and every high thing that exalts itself against the knowledge of God, and bringing into captivity every thought to the obedience of Christ; And having in a readiness to revenge all disobedience, when your obedience is fulfilled." 2 Corinthians 10:4-7

Remember, the battlefield is in our minds. Thus, **the 1st *weapon I will discuss is an awareness of evil and the knowledge of God*.** You must know what the scripture says so you can use it when you are being attacked. Jesus did this when he said, "It is written" in his wilderness temptations. The other thing is to know when you are being attacked. If you are married and looking at another girl to lust, you are being tempted i.e. attacked. If you don't know that, you will indulge yourself in immoral fantasies and end up a captive of the devil.

If you have the knowledge of God, you can use it as a weapon. Here's an example: "Thou shalt not commit adultery" You can use it to cast down your imagination. It is just a matter of speaking out what it is that is written. This action will cast down the imagination or anything else that tries to set itself up above the knowledge that God has given you.

If your obedience is up to date, you will be ready to take revenge against the evil spirit that brings the imagination to you. You will realize that it is just another fiery dart being shot at you to lead you astray.

All this can go on in your mind in seconds and never manifest in reality… or you can linger on the lustful array of thoughts and slide downward into the abyss of pornography and actual attempts to live out your immorality.

Using the knowledge of God as a weapon is crucial to your self-defense. Knowing the tricks of the devil and the insurrection of the Beast within will keep you from failing in your faith and damaging your relationship with your Heavenly Father.

The next weapon is the **"Peace of God**. "And let the peace of God rule in your hearts, to the which also ye are called in one body; and be ye thankful." Colossians 3:15

Remember, we are playing mind games with the rulers of darkness. The best way to avoid evil traps is to use the peace of God as a weapon. Here's how it works.

You have been offered a new job but the company has a reputation of being shady. It will mean more money and better hours. However, this company has a history of abuse with employees and the general public. What do you do? Your gut tells you to stay away from it. But your mind says to take it because of the money. The trick is to ask yourself, "How do you feel about it and how does God feel about it." No peace, no can do.

When you read the word, "Let" in the scriptures, it means to allow. That is a choice you will have to make. You need to listen to the feelings and allow them to rule or referee in the situation.

Most of these weapons are suitable for use against the attacks of the devil and the beast within.

Our next weapon is the name of Jesus. Hear what the Bible says, "That at the name of Jesus every knee should bow, of things in heaven, and things in earth, and things under the earth; And that every tongue should confess that Jesus Christ is Lord, to the glory of God the Father." Philippians 2:10-11

Here are a few other references to the name of Jesus:

Acts 4:12 - Neither is there salvation in any other: for there is none other name under heaven given among men, whereby we must be saved.

John 14:13 - And whatsoever ye shall ask in my name, that will I do, that the Father may be glorified in the Son.

Romans 10:13 - For whosoever shall call upon the name of the Lord shall be saved.

1 Corinthians 6:11 - And such were some of you: but ye are washed, but ye are sanctified, but ye are justified in the name of the Lord Jesus, and by the Spirit of our God.

Acts 2:38 - Then Peter said unto them, Repent, and be baptized every one of you in the name of Jesus Christ for the remission of sins, and ye shall receive the gift of the Holy Ghost.

Mark 16:17 - And these signs shall follow them that believe; In my name shall they cast out devils; they shall speak with new tongues;

John 14:6 - Jesus saith unto him, I am the way, the truth, and the life: no man cometh unto the Father, but by me.

When you use the name of Jesus, you are speaking in the language of the Spirit. Say it out loud with me. IN THE NAME OF JESUS. Speak it out and all of heaven and even hell listens. They do so because they all must bow to his Lordship. Even demons have to flee.

You can stand up against evil spirits, sickness, despair and even circumstances that are oppressive.

However, there is one condition to being victorious in your good fight of faith. It is found in revelation 12:11 "And **they overcame him** by the **blood** of the Lamb, **and** by the word of their testimony; and **they** loved not their lives unto the death."

They (Believers) overcame (Victory) him (devil) by the blood of the lamb (death of Jesus on the cross), the word of their testimony (being "Born

45

Again" children of God) and because they loved NOT their lives unto the death. (their priority was Jesus and his power to deliver) They died to any self-ambition and glory and concentrated on winning the battle.

I see this like a soldier that is in a battle against an opposing army. He does not think of maybe getting a medal for his valor. He rather fights to survive and win the day. If he must die, he must. But that's all part of the fighting. This is what is called, "Good Courage."

Another weapon is The Blood of Jesus. The above scripture includes the blood of Jesus as one of the ways the saints overcame. It's ok to speak directly to an evil spirit, saying, "I come against you with the Blood of Jesus." It is the blood that cleanses us from all unrighteousness. I John 1:9. It is also ok to bind that evil spirit by the blood of Christ, saying to the devil, "You are defeated by the blood and I use it now to block your attack and strip you of any power you may have over me or my family…now lose me and get out of my life"

The 1st century was full of followers of Jesus. There were also disciples of Christ. The difference between them was, "What's in it for me?" The followers never got involved. They were on-lookers, watching to see what would happen next. The disciples were not only followers but serious students of his teachings to apply them in their lives. Jesus did not say, go and make followers. He, just before ascending into heaven said, "Therefore go and make disciples of all nations, baptizing them in the name of the Father and of the Son and of the Holy Spirit, and teaching them to obey everything I have commanded you. And surely, I am with you always, to the very end of the age." Matthew 28:19-20

Disciples are taught to obey the teachings of Christ. That becomes a lifestyle, not a religion or passing fad. If we are a disciple, we are committed to his teaching and using the weapons he has provided.

The next weapon is the "Sword of the Spirit." The sword of the Spirit is mentioned in Ephesians 6:17: "take the helmet of salvation, and the **sword of the Spirit, which is the word of God**."

This sword is the last piece of armor Paul describes in talking about the armor of God and is the only offensive weapon depicted. Scripture tells us that the sword of the Spirit is the Word of God. But what exactly is the Word of God, and why is it effective?

The Bible says this about that: "For the word of God is quick, and powerful, and sharper than any two-edged sword, piercing even to the dividing asunder of soul and spirit, and of the joints and marrow, and is a discerner of the thoughts and intents of the heart." Hebrews 4:12 The word of God is another term used to describe the Bible.

So, when you quote or otherwise use the scriptures, you are flashing the Sword of the Spirit. You have every right to use it in self-defense to fight off evil spirits, temptation, depression, oppression or any other attack. This is what Jesus did when he said, "It is written. "What was written" Over 3,000 promises of God to mankind in multiple covenants and open statements through the centuries.

If we speak the Word, we also hear the Word and that generates faith that will ultimately move mountains. Here's two scriptures to support my premise:

- "So then, faith cometh by hearing and hearing by the word of God." Romans 10:13
- So Jesus said to them, "Surely, I say to you, if you have faith as a mustard seed, you will say to this mountain, 'Move from here to there,' and it will move; and nothing will be impossible for you" Matthew 17:20 NKJ Version

The Sword of the Spirit can be used for both offensive and defensive purposes as indicated in the scriptures above. It is important, however, to realize that when the scriptures say that the sword is the "Word", it is saying that it is the same "Word" that the apostle John spoke of in his gospel. "In the beginning was the "Word", and the "Word" was with God, and the "Word" was God. He was in the beginning with God. All things were made through him, and without him was not anything made that was made. In him was life, and the life was the light of men." John 1:1-4

This is the same "Word" that John says became flesh. "And the

"Word" became flesh and dwelt among us and we have seen his glory, glory as of the only Son from the Father, full of grace and truth. John 1:14

This is the same "Word" that Paul says is the Sword of the Spirit" that is now available to us to use as a defense and as an offensive weapon to battle the rulers of darkness. This means that all that Jesus is, is all that we need to fight the good fight of faith. He is, The Way, The Truth, The Life. John 14:6 He is characterized by being a two-edged sword that knows the intent of every heart. Hebrews 4:12

If we apply the teaching of Jesus, we will be using the Sword of the Spirit. We can tear down strongholds, break apart chains and chase demons away by wheeling the sword (Word) in the face of danger. Here's how it works: The Word says all things work together for good to those who reverence God and are called according to his purposes. Romans 8:28

When we are in a thing that is difficult, beyond our control or overwhelming, we can apply Romans 8:28 saying, this thing will work out for my good because I honor God and have been called by him to fulfil his purposes here on earth.

The Word is alive in us because we are "Born Again" and it will do what it has said in the Bible....work all things together for good. This brings peace in the midst of confusion and turmoil. It brings comfort to our weary souls and it will literally cause our reality to coincide with the will of God.

Now let's go back to the armor of God spoken of in Ephesians 6: "Wherefore take unto you the **whole armor of God**, that ye may be able to withstand in the evil day, and having done all, to stand. Stand therefore, having your **loins girt about with truth**, and having on **the breastplate of righteousness**; and your **feet shod with the preparation of the gospel of peace**; Above all, taking **the shield of faith**, wherewith ye shall be able to quench all the fiery darts of the wicked. And take **the helmet of salvation,** and **the sword of the Spirit**, which is the word of God: Praying always with all prayer and supplication in the Spirit, and watching thereunto with all perseverance and supplication for all saints; Ephesians 6:13-18

This is the armor of God given to every Christian. He expects us to wear it every day. Let's look at the parts of the uniform.

1. *loins girt about with truth...* the **sides between the lower ribs and pelvis, and the lower part of the back.**

2. *the breastplate of righteousness...* a piece of armor covering the chest.

3. *feet shod with the preparation of the gospel of peace...* A good pair of shoes allows the soldier to be ready for conflict.

4. *the shield of faith...* a device or part that serves as a protective cover or barrier.

5. *the helmet of salvation...* a covering or enclosing headpiece of ancient or medieval armor.

6. *the sword of the Spirit...* a two-edged sword symbolizing the Word of God that can discern and destroy evil.

So, we can see from the armor that we are fully protected against evil forces. Paul tells us that all of this armor is necessary so we can stand in the day of evil. He says, having done all, to stand. Stand therefore. He didn't say compromise, fall apart with fear, run for the hills or surrender. He said we can stand or withstand anything that the devil throws at us.

Points of clarification: A breastplate of righteousness is not us being righteous. It is rather the awareness that we are the righteousness of God in Christ Jesus. See it for yourself.

"God made him who had no sin to be sin for us, so that in him we might become the righteousness of God" (2 Corinthians 5:21). This is an amazing truth. The devil will say that we are not righteous and can never be good enough but that lie cannot penetrate our breastplate.

A shield of Faith is a covering made to shield you from the fiery darts of Satan. When we fight the good fight of faith, we must raise our faith-filled shield in defense of our sanity, our peace, our happiness and all that is ours. It will quench the fiery darts and spoil the attack.

When we shod our feet, we wear a good pair of shoes, suitable for battle.

This is necessary to stand when fighting. Paul uses the preparation of the gospel of peace as the pair of shoes we are to wear. This is to say, prepare by studying, memorizing scripture and being ready to quote certain passages that apply to your situation. We must know what the gospel says and have it at our fingertips at all times.

Fighting Demonic Spirits

When we discuss fighting demonic spirits, it is easy to fall into error. One error is that we begin to believe that there's a demon behind every situation. That is just not so. It is easy to say, *"The devil Made Me Do It"* instead of owning up to our own lust, anger or other failures.

People have a "Free Will" to make decisions and they often times use poor judgment and make wrong decisions that can affect others. Blaming demons is popular because it hides the evil in our own hearts. "The heart is deceitful above all things, and desperately wicked: who can know it" **Jeremiah 17:9**

Jesus said, "Not that which goes into the mouth defiles a man, but that which cometh out of the mouth, this defiles a man." **Mathew 15:11** So blaming evil forces for what we do is not religiously correct.

The other error in fighting demonic influences is…not believing that demonic activity is real and that it never affects you. Jesus cast out demons. His disciples did also and for centuries the church has faced demonic activity.

Here's a partial list of situations that might indicate that you are under demonic control or attack.

- Thinking thoughts "that are not yours."
- Having sudden depression.
- Having suicidal thoughts.
- Having fits of anger or rage that are unusual for you.
- Feeling hopeless.
- Your pets start acting differently around you.

- Your close friends start questioning your thinking or behavior.

- Excessive fatigue.

- Not being able to do what you know is good or right.

- Feeling like you are being pulled to do the wrong thing.

- Feeling like you are being pressured to do something you don't want to do.

- Hearing voices or thoughts in your head that are negative, persuasive or commanding you to do something.

- Deep or severe personality changes like fear or wanting to be isolated all the time.

- Suddenly having creepy or scary feelings.

- Recent feelings that an area, like in your house, there is something heavy, depressive or oppressive.

- Feelings of being under attack or threatened when others don't.

- Finding it hard or impossible to pray.

- Finding it harder or impossible to spend time with Christian brothers or sisters.

- Sudden and unexplainable anxiety.

- Sudden development of Lupus or other auto immune system decease.

Some medical problems can cause similar conditions. It could be from a new bad habit or an encounter with a sinful situation or circumstance. If this is true, you know what to do. Repent and move on with your life. Trust Jesus. (The above list is an excerpt from Pastor Thomas of The Joseph Plan World Wide Ministry) ministry@thejosephplan.org

The best way to dispel demonic activity in your life is to call upon the name of the Lord and command that demons to leave you, ***in the name of Jesus***. Then draw close to God, through prayer and seek his divine revelation as to what to do next.

He will most likely send you to his Word to read and listen as he speaks to you from the pages of the bible. You will get all the direction you need to overcome and demonic influence.

Remember, Resist the devil and he will flee from you. To resist is to quote scripture, as Jesus did when he was in the wilderness.

If you are like me, you probably said, *"Why Me Lord."* There was a time when I thought I could be neutral, just doing my own thing but still believing in God. The problem with that sort of thinking is that cannot be.

We were created to be the image and likeness of God here on this earth. God went to a lot of trouble to create and enact a plan that would accomplish this. With the fall of Adam and the entire human race, we were left with being the image of Satan. Now our "Free Will" choice is to stay with the deeds of the flesh, which is the nature of evil or to be, "Born Again" and receive the Spirit of God. There is no neutral ground.

There are some believers who falsely believe that if they have a lot of faith, they will not undergo any suffering, severe tests or satanic attacks. Nothing could be further from the truth! Actually, the opposite is true.

I Peter 5:8-9 teaches that Satan roams the earth seeking someone to devour. When we read the context, we can come to the conclusion that the devil's main focus is to distract and disarm the children of God. Consequently, when someone on earth wants to bring the influence of the kingdom of God on earth as it is in heaven, Satan fights back to keep the earth under his control.

This is why it seems as though a person following the will of God will sometimes have the most difficult tests, trials and resistance, as opposed to some saints who are casual seekers of God.

Satan is no dummy, why should he attack a Christian who is a bad example to others and who is already deceived and in his grip? He will focus rather on those who are the biggest threat to his authority and rule Remember: God gave Adam a commission to have his rule over the whole earth (Gen. 1:28), and immediately after that the devil came and convinced both Adam and Eve to disobey God and abandon their posts as God's voice reigns over the earth **(Gen. 3:1-8).**

Since that time Satan has been jealously attempting to protect his control over the earthly realm which he stole through subverting Adam, including its systems of government, commerce, media, the arts, science and education.

Those who attempt to bring Gods' influence in these areas will most likely experience some of the highest levels of satanic resistance. The apostle Paul had a messenger from Satan follow him everywhere he went that caused riots and persecutions **(2 Cor. 13:1-8),** only because he was turning the present world system upside down **(Acts 17:7).**

So, if you are sold out for God, don't be discouraged when you are attacked or allow yourself to be deceived into thinking that the only reason you are in intense spiritual warfare or tribulation is because you may have missed God. It may be the opposite. You are being targeted because you are hitting the divine bulls-eye! This is why Paul admonished believers to stand strong in the Lord: "Our struggle is not against flesh and blood but against principalities, powers and the rulers of darkness in high places" **(Ephesians 6:10-13).**

Notice: Paul said "our struggle" meaning he was including himself in this struggle. Every time there was an open door for ministry, he had many adversaries. This is a Biblical principle **(read 1 Corinthians 16:9).**

Do not ever think that just because God is calling you to do something that it will be easy. Jesus did the will of God and he was crucified, and church history tells us Paul was beheaded! It's not how many years we live, but what we do with the years we are alive… that matters!

So, what do we do when we are in a time of spiritual warfare that Paul calls "the day of evil" in Ephesians 6:13? Paul tells us in this passage to be strong in the Lord and to stand firm; in other words, do not quit (Eph. 6:10-13). This is fighting the good fight of faith

The apostle Peter also tells us to resist the devil, standing firm in the faith (1 Pet. 5:9). Peter knew firsthand that faith in God is the key to standing firm in the midst of the day of evil because, when he denied Christ three times, Jesus prayed for him that his "faith" would not fail (Luke 22:31-32).

So, do not be afraid when you are in tribulation, because Jesus has already overcome the world (John 16:33)!

We are privileged to stand up for our faith and belief in Jesus Christ. We should take every opportunity to share our faith and stand for what is right, no matter what others think.

The Bible gives us clear instruction on how to keep ourselves free, healthy and happy in a world that is a battleground where Satan seeks to kill, steal and destroy. (John 10:10) Here's a recap of what we can do next to keep our hearts:

Be transformed-...Romans 12:2; Cast down imaginations-...2 Corinthians 10:5; Bring into captivity every thought to the obedience of Christ; 2 Corinthians 10:5; Be spiritually minded-Romans 8:6; Put off the old man-Ephesians 4:22; Be renewed in your mind-Ephesians 4:23; Put on the new man-Ephesians 4:24; Let the mind of Christ be in you- Philippians 5; Let no man beguile you-Colossians 2:18; Let no man spoil you-Colossians 2:8; Be fully persuaded in your mind-Romans 14:5; Do not have a doubtful mind-Luke 12:29; Do not be soon shaken in mind-2 Thessalonians 2:2; Do not Be troubled-2 Thessalonians 2:2; Gird up the loins of your mind-1 Peter 1:13; Be sober-1 Peter 1:13 and above all Hope to the end for the grace of God-1 Peter.

Being good and doing the right things in life can empower you and keep you strong in the Lord. Here are a few things that can be called *a weapon of righteousness*. Some have already been mentioned but I thought it was appropriate to name them again so you can see how righteous living can be weaponized to your benefit.

1. The Bible.... All God's words are true and righteous (Psalm 119:160, 172) and useful for "training in righteousness" (2 Timothy 3:16). That makes the Bible an effective weapon for Christians.

"For the word of God is alive and active. Sharper than any double-edged sword, it penetrates even to dividing soul and spirit, joints and marrow; it judges the thoughts and attitudes of the heart" (Hebrews 4:12). Jesus used God's Word to defeat Satan's temptations (Matthew 4:1–11).

The word of the Lord is pictured as a sword coming out of his mouth, having power to strike down the nations (Revelation 19:15, 21). God's Word is one of the "weapons of righteousness" against the forces of evil.

2. Faith.... The Old Testament tells of heroes "who through faith conquered kingdoms, administered justice, and gained what was promised; who shut the mouths of lions, quenched the fury of the flames, and escaped the edge of the sword; whose weakness was turned into strength; and who became powerful in battle and routed foreign armies" (Hebrews 11:33–34).

This should not surprise us, since Jesus revealed that even a small amount of faith has enough power to move mountains (Matthew 17:20). "Everyone born of God overcomes the world. This is the victory that has overcome the world, even our faith" (1 John 5:4).

3. Prayer.... "The prayer of a righteous person is powerful and effective" (James 5:16). Scripture is full of examples of the power of prayer. Summarizing the time of the judges, Nehemiah 9:27 says, "When they were oppressed, they cried out to you. From heaven, you heard them and in your great compassion you gave them deliverers, who rescued them from the hand of their enemies."

By prayer the drought was begun and ended during Elijah's day (James 5:17–18). By prayer the enemies of Elisha were struck blind (2 Kings 6:18). By prayer Samson achieved victory over the Philistines (Judges 16:28–30).

4. Goodness.... Goodness is another weapon of righteousness. We are instructed to "overcome evil with good" (Romans 12:21).

Sometimes it seems that evil is more powerful, or at least more prevalent, but it is only temporary. One believer, taking a stand on the side of goodness, can turn back much evil. It is important that we "add to our faith goodness," which empowers us to defeat the evil of the world and the evil within our own sin nature (2 Peter 1:4–5).

Love.... All our other weapons of righteousness are worthless without this one, the greatest commandment (Mark 12:30–31); it is even greater than faith (1 Corinthians 13:1–3). It is a fruit of the Holy Spirit (Galatians 5:22). **"For God hath not given us the spirit of fear; but of power, and of love, and of a sound mind."** (2 Timothy 1:7).

5. Love empowers Christians by uniting them, giving them understanding, encouragement, and joy (Colossians 2:2–3; Philemon 1:4–7). We are to trust in God's love, and it will protect us from evil (Psalm 17:7; 5 2:8; 61:7) just as surely as it cleansed us from sin and defeated Satan's plans against us (Psalm 103:10–12; John 3:16; Revelation 12:10).

In addition to the weapons of righteousness, Christians are supplied with the "full armor of God" to empower us mere humans to stand against Satan himself and all the forces of hell (Ephesians 6:10–17).

Our protective gear includes the breastplate of righteousness, the helmet of salvation, and the shield of faith, plus one offensive weapon, our sword, the Word of God (verse 17). We, the church, are to be on the offense, God's army against whom the gates of hell cannot prevail (Matthew 16:18).

War is marked by death. Our Savior conquered death, then gave to us that same power over death and all other threats. Therefore, "we are more than conquerors through him who loved us.

For I am convinced that neither death nor life, neither angels nor demons, neither the present nor the future, nor any powers, neither height nor depth, nor anything else in all creation, will be able to separate us from the love of God that is in Christ Jesus our Lord." Romans 8:37–39 (Excerpts from gotquestions.com)

I am sure you will find more things as you read the scripture but these will make a great starting place. Just remember, God is always with you. He is not mad at you, nor does he expect you to win every time. Your salvation does not hang in the balance. If you fail, he will just pick you up and help you along the way until you can sit, walk and stand in faith.

With the weapons of righteousness for the right hand and for the left. 2 Corinthians 6:7 The phrase, "weapons of righteousness," sometimes translated as, "armor of righteousness," has been interpreted many ways, from the plausible to the ludicrous. These weapons are often linked to our spiritual armor found in Ephesians 6. Though I do believe there is likely some link to the armor of God, I believe John Calvin was closer to the mark when he linked these weapons to holy conduct and a clear conscience. Understanding it in this way, we can see them as both armor and weapons.

Nothing can hinder us in our work for the Lord more than sin and a troubled conscience. In both of these things, we find ourselves exposed to the attacks of Satan and unable to work to advance the kingdom of God. However, with a righteous life and a clear conscience, we can stand in the midst of adversity and persecution.

The real problem is that in and of ourselves, we have neither. We are guilty and we know it, but in Jesus we find our forgiveness and acceptance. Jesus is the foundation of our armor and weapons of righteousness. None of us have any ability or right to stand in truthful speech and the power of God unless we are in Christ, but with him we can stand with our conscious clear, justified by his blood.

From there we must grow in sanctification. This means we are not only declared righteous, but we also begin to be conformed to his image. If we plan to stand against the rulers off darkness and the patterns of this world, both justification and sanctification are necessary.

As we grow in the Lord, we become able to work to advance the kingdom of God without any fault being found in our work. We must put aside underhanded ways (2 Cor. 4:2). In this way we can press on in the face of any mistreatment, knowing that we have conducted ourselves according to the word of God.

It is only with these weapons of righteousness that we can stand as servants of God and commend ourselves in every way: by great endurance, in afflictions, hardships, calamities, beatings, imprisonments, riots, labors, sleepless nights, hunger; by purity, knowledge, patience, kindness, the Holy Spirit, genuine love; by truthful speech, and the power of God; with the weapons of righteousness for the right hand and for the left; through honor and dishonor, through slander and praise. Treated as impostors, and yet true; as punished, and yet not killed; as sorrowful, yet always rejoicing; as poor, yet making many rich; as having nothing, yet possessing everything with our hearts wide open (2 Cor. 6:4-11).

Paul concludes the weapons with, "Praying Always" with all prayer and supplication in the Spirit. We must communicate with the Holy Spirit at all times in order to get fresh revelation and new direction as we engage in spiritual warfare.

CHAPTER FIVE:

WHAT IS OUR BATTLE STRATEGY?

Our Battle strategy comes directly from the pages of the Bible. It is the final authority. I use the Bible as my main source to validate all that I say. But most people, including Christians, do not read the Bible with any regularity and therefore do not know the God of the Bible. They know only what their pastor or others tell them. Here's a brief history lesson.

The history of the Bible starts with a phenomenal account, the creation of all things. It's not one book like many think -- It's an ancient collection of writings, comprised of 66 separate books, written over approximately 1,600 years, by at least 40 distinct authors. The Old Testament contains 39 books written from approximately 1500 BC to 400 BC, and the New Testament contains 27 books written from approximately 40 to 90 AD. The Jewish Bible (*Tanakh*) is the same as the Christian Old Testament, except for its book arrangement. The original Old Testament was written mainly in Hebrew, with some Aramaic, while the original New Testament was written in common Greek.

Starting in about 40 AD, and continuing to about 90 AD, the eye-witnesses to the life of Jesus, including Matthew, Mark, Luke, John, Paul, James, Peter and Jude, wrote the Gospels and letters that eventually became the Bible's New Testament. These authors quote from 31 books of the Old Testament.

They widely circulated their material so that by about 150 AD, early Christians were referring to the entire set of writings as the "New Covenant." During the 200s AD, the original writings were translated from Greek into Latin, Coptic (Egypt) and Syriac (Syria), and widely disseminated as "Inspired Scripture" throughout the Roman Empire and beyond. In 397

AD, in an effort to protect the scriptures from various heresies and offshoot religious movements, the current 27 books of the New Testament were formally and finally confirmed and "canonized" in the Synod of Carthage.

What I hope you will see from this snapshot of the Bible in history is that God took great pains to validate his Word to man over many years, keeping it clear, and indisputable as the only true source of his revelation. These eyewitness accounts and prophetic revelations all connect to make a complete proof of God's existence, character, power, love, salvation, judgment, compassion, mercy and forgiveness. His entire plan of salvation and the ages to come are all written down so we could benefit from them.

Time and time again I have asked the Lord questions and found the answers in the Bible. I can remember one in particular.

I was attending a small Christian fellowship that met in a barn. The leadership was teaching that God's judgment upon America was to come soon and that they could escape it by leaving the states and going to a remote desert-like place in another country. Several families had already moved to this undisclosed location. I was a very young believer and not as knowledgeable as I am now in the scriptures…so I turned to Jesus and asked him if these people were correct and if I should go with them. Here's what I read during my prayer and Bible reading.

Mathew 24:26 "Wherefore if they shall say unto you, Behold, he is in the desert; go not forth: behold, he is in the secret chambers; believe it not."

This is just one example of many that God has communicated to me through the Bible. Try it…when you are troubled, confused or worried about life or just need an answer to life's never-ending questions, pray and ask Jesus to show you in his Word, the Bible.

The Bible was written under "Inspiration" from the Holy Spirit. The word, "inspire" means "To breathe upon or into something". God revealed himself through individuals who penned the written word.

As a young Christian, I often witnessed to un-believers, using the Bible as my source. Some of those I talked to told me that the Bible was not a source they would believe. I went to my pastor and asked him what I should do because folks were not open to hear what the Bible had to say.

He led me to **Hebrews 4:12** and said. "Use it anyway," for the reasons stated in chapter four. Listen to what it says. "For the word of God is quick, and powerful, and sharper than any two-edged sword, piercing even to the dividing asunder of soul and spirit, and of the joints and marrow, and is a discerner of the thoughts and intents of the heart." **(Hebrews 4:12)** I did just that and began to see the words of the Bible break down barriers and soften hearts.

I know that anyone who is really seeking God and wants to know about Jesus will find everything in the Bible. Words will leap off the page, bringing fresh revelation, historical facts, wisdom, divine counsel and victory over life's every trial. All you have to do is spend some time every day in prayer and Bible reading.

There is always a battle strategy. You cannot go to war without one. I was once told that failing to plan is planning to fail. We really need to design a plan that will act as a guide to take us through the battle. We need some sort of, "What to do" strategy.

I spent many years as a sales & marketing executive and learned first-hand the art of overcoming objections. I designed a guide for new sales people that was in fact a situational strategy manual. It posed a question as to why the prospect would not buy and offered an answer.

Designing a situational strategy manual is the same for those that are caught without an answer to the devil's suggestion. For example: There is nothing wrong with having a live-in girlfriend that participates in sexual experiences. Society says sex before marriage is a good thing. Who can say it wrong?

The truth is, God says it is wrong. Hear what the Bible says about fornication. It's the Biblical word for sexual immorality, sex before marriage:

1 Corinthians 6:18-20 - Flee fornication. Every sin that a man doeth is without the body; but he that committeth fornication sins against his own body.

Hebrews 13:4 - Marriage is honorable in all, and the bed undefiled: but whoremongers and adulterers God will judge.

Galatians 5:19-21 - Now the works of the flesh are manifest, which are these; Adultery, fornication, uncleanness, lasciviousness, and so on.

1 Corinthians 7:2 - Nevertheless, to avoid fornication, let every man have his own wife, and let every woman have her own husband.

Revelation 21:8 - But the fearful, and unbelieving, and the abominable, and murderers, and whoremongers, and sorcerers, and idolaters, and all liars, shall have their part in the lake which burns with fire and brimstone: which is the second death.

Matthew 5:32 - But I say unto you, that whosoever shall put away his wife, saving for the cause of fornication, causes her to commit adultery: and whosoever shall marry her that is divorced committeth adultery.

1 Corinthians 6:9-11 - Know ye not that the unrighteous shall not inherit the kingdom of God? Be not deceived: neither fornicators, nor idolaters, nor adulterers, nor effeminate, nor abusers of themselves with mankind,

1 Corinthians 6:13 - Meats for the belly, and the belly for meats: but God shall destroy both it and them. Now the body is not for fornication, but for the Lord; and the Lord for the body.

1 Thessalonians 4:3-4 - For this is the will of God, even your sanctification, that ye should abstain from fornication:

Knowing the word of God gives you the truth and an edge over the lies. You can overcome the immorality of the day by stating the truth against it. This is having a battle strategy.

I know what you are going to say. You might say, "No one will listen to me. I am not a Bible scholar. No, you are not a scholar. Neither am I. We are, however, led by the Spirit of God by divine truth. Who cares what others think or say. Saying or speaking the truth can be just in your mind to keep you safe from a clear and present danger. But there will be times that it is necessary to speak the truth before others to set the record straight and let them know you have values.

Here are a few situations that will require you to build a strategy that will overcome the intent and success of evil.

- Evolution is the basis for all life on earth.
- Homosexuality is just an alternate lifestyle.
- Pornography is really an art form.
- If I am a good person, God will let me into his heaven.
- All religions lead folks to God. There is not just one way.
- Sex before marriage is ok if both are consenting adults.
- Taking drugs like cocaine and weed is ok because they are recreational.
- Fraudulent activity is ok if it just hurts insurance companies.
- Cheating on a spouse is an acceptable practice if the marriage is floundering.
- Lying to a friend or parent is ok if it is just a "White" lie.
- Thievery is ok too if it is committed by a homeless person.
- Salvation is not by grace but rather by works.
- Our church is the true church. All others are false.
- Our religion is the true religion.
- The Bible is just an old history book that has no relevance for today.
- Jesus was a prophet but he was not God.
- Man is inherently good. He does not need to be saved.
- We are all children of God, no matter what race or religion.

This is enough to get you started in development of Biblical strategies. The goal here is to offer a rebuttal for each of the above based upon the word of God. Why is what has been said untrue? That is the essence of any rebuttal.

The last point I want to share is "Faith" and how it works in spiritual warfare and self-defense. Most of us know the famous scripture that defines faith. It is found in Hebrews. "Now faith is the substance of things hoped for, the evidence of things not seen." Hebrews 11:1

What does that mean and how does it apply to my daily lifestyle? Best I can figure, faith is the substance and the evidence of what I am hoping for. The fact that it is unseen is because I am still hoping for it. It has not appeared in my life as yet. However, I can look to my faith as my proof that it will appear in God's timing. My faith will actually bring it into existence.

So what is faith? It is, in my humble opinion, the ability to believe. I believe that God will answer my prayers and my provision will come forth. Did not Jesus say, "And all things, whatsoever ye shall ask in prayer, believing, ye shall receive." Matthew 21:22

Here are a few more scripture references to Faith.

Mark 11:24 KJV...Therefore I say unto you, What things soever ye desire, when ye pray, believe that ye receive them, and ye shall have them.

Matthew 17:20 KJV...And Jesus said unto them, verily I say unto you, If ye have faith as a grain of mustard seed, ye shall say unto this mountain, Remove hence to yonder place; and it shall remove; and nothing shall be impossible unto you.

Matthew 21:21 KJV...Jesus answered and said unto them, Verily I say unto you, If ye have faith, and doubt not, ye shall not only do this which is done to the fig tree, but also if ye shall say unto this mountain, Be thou removed, and be thou cast into the sea; it shall be done.

Hebrews 11:6 KJV...But without faith it is impossible to please him: for he that cometh to God must believe that he is, and that he is a rewarder of them that diligently seek him.

John 8:24 KJV...I said therefore unto you, that ye shall die in your sins: for if ye believe not that I am he, ye shall die in your sins.

Ephesians 3:16-17 KJV...That he would grant you, according to the riches of his glory, to be strengthened with might by his Spirit in the inner man; That Christ may dwell in your hearts by faith; that ye, being rooted and grounded in love.

Romans 10:17 KJV...So then faith cometh by hearing, and hearing by the word of God.

Romans 15:13 KJV...Now the God of hope fill you with all joy and peace in believing, that ye may abound in hope, through the power of the Holy Ghost.

It all boils down to believing God and trusting that what he said will come to pass in your life.

CHAPTER SIX:

CAN WE OPT-OUT AND NOT FIGHT?

Some folks have questioned the need to fight. They have no interest in battling the rulers of darkness. Well, there is a free will granted to all of us and that means you can opt-out if you want. If fact, millions have done just that. They have strayed from the truth to follow strange teachings that are not biblical.

According to the PEW report on trends in Christianity, the church is confused about basic doctrine. There is statistical data that reveals how folks believe that call themselves Christians. Here's a quick overview.

Americans Are Divided on Whether Jesus Was Sinless. Perhaps reflective of their questions about Jesus' divinity, Americans are conflicted on whether Jesus committed sins during his earthly life. About half of Americans agree, either strongly or somewhat, that while he lived on earth, Jesus Christ was human and committed sins like other people (52%).

Similar to other trends in perceptions of Jesus, Millennials are more likely to believe Jesus committed sins while he was on earth—56% of Millennials believe so. Gen-Xers, Boomers and Elders are all similar to the national average when it comes to beliefs about Jesus' fallibility—they are almost evenly split on whether Jesus sinned while he lived on earth.

Most Americans Say They Have Made a Commitment to Jesus Christ.

On the whole, America is still committed to Jesus. The act of making a personal commitment to Jesus—often seen as the "first step" in becoming a Christian—is a step that more than six in ten Americans say they have taken and, moreover, that commitment is still important in their life today. **People Are Conflicted between "Jesus" and "Good Deeds" as the Way to Heaven.**

Overall, roughly two out of five Americans have confessed their sinfulness and professed faith in Christ (a group Barna classifies as "born again Christians").

Why all the statistics? Simple, so you can see the condition of the church. Their beliefs are all over the place. 44% do not believe Jesus was God in the flesh. If this is not a falling away, I don't know what is.

A false Christian is one who says he or she is a Christian but was never, "Born Again." The Church is slowly trending toward a unity that excludes personal faith and fundamental doctrines. Instead, they follow salvation by works, acceptance of immoral open sin among members and a general lack of Godliness.

Jesus said that there would be a falling away from the faith before he returns. It's happening now in our lifetime. The Bible says it will keep declining.

16% of Christians do not believe in God.

53% of Christians do not attend church even once per week.

47% of Christians seldom attend prayer groups.

35% of Christians do not feel a sense of spiritual peace or wellbeing.

22% of Christians believe that God, The Father, is greater than Jesus.

The apostle John, among other writers in the New Testament, mentions certain characteristics of the Anti-Christ. In the first place, there is the Anti-Christ with a capital "A." There were also many anti-Christ's in the world at the time of the New Testament church with a lower-case "a."

What is the difference between these two? Did the writers of the New Testament make a mistake in their choosing between a lower-case "a" and an upper-case "A?"

No, they were simply pointing out that anyone that opposes, for example, the divinity of Christ is an anti-Christ. There are many out there today who are anti-Christs in that they deny the deity of Jesus Christ who is God (John 1).

Unbelievably, many who graduate from seminary deny that Jesus was fully God and fully man. These, by definition, are anti-Christs. Atheists could be said to be anti-Christ because they do not believe in God and thus Jesus Christ as God and so they stand condemned (John 3:18).

These anti-Christs are not one person but a spirit of anti-Christ and so we know that there are many anti-Christs but it is the spirit of anti-Christ that lives within humans and not a specific person (2 John 4:3).

In 1 John 2:18 John makes a distinction regarding the anti-Christ as he wrote, "Children, it is the last hour, and as you have heard that Anti-Christ is coming, so now many anti-Christs have come. Therefore, we know that it is the last hour." Here John states that there are many anti-Christs and that "you have heard that Anti-Christ is coming."

John continues in verse 22, "Who is the liar? It is whoever denies that Jesus is the Christ. Such a person is the anti-Christ, denying the Father and the Son." Here again the identity of the lower-case anti-Christ is anyone who denies that Jesus is the Christ.

The Christ means the *anointed One of God.* As John says, whoever denies Jesus as the Christ, or as the Messiah, denies the Father and the Son and this person and these people are the anti-Christs." There are many anti-Christs out there today just as there were in John's Day. But the anti-Christs are not the same as the Anti-Christ, upper-case "A." The world has no shortage of anti-Christs.

Their characteristics are that they also deny his virgin birth, his resurrection, his living a sinless life, and that he will return again to judge the world. For the believer, he will come as their King. For those who reject his gospel, he will come as their Judge (Rev 20). Either way, everyone will bow the knee and acknowledge Jesus Christ as Lord. Both condemned sinners and resurrected and glorified saints (Rom 14:11, Phil 2:10).

It is hard for me to believe that folks that call themselves Christians can be numbered among the anti-Christs. These could even be those that teach our kids in Sunday school, preach from the pulpit and influence church policies.

Yes, you can opt-out of the fight and become as one of those that have fallen away from true faith into a false sense of security. You will, however, still be attacked by evil forces and led by the Beast within (the Anti-Christ) down the broad road that leads to destruction and eternal damnation.

It's much better to fight the good fight of faith, win the battle and glorify God in the process.

CHAPTER SEVEN:
WHAT IS THE GOOD FIGHT OF FAITH?

Fighting the good fight of faith simply means that we will not consider Christ's sacrifice as nothing. Fighting the good fight of faith means that we will value what Christ has given to us higher than any other thing in this universe, even larger than our very lives and we will fight for it, no matter what.

Fighting the good fight of faith is to be steadfast in our beliefs with no compromise when faced with false doctrines, fake Christians and persecution form liberals that serve the god of this world.

Fighting the good fight of faith is about **making a choice;** a choice to pursue God's will and a life of faith on a daily basis. It is about deciding to fight the temptations and factors that pull away from God and instead lean into him.

Paul specifies it's about the Christian faith and the battle ground for the fight is about preserving the faith just like Jude wrote, "contend for the faith that was once for all delivered to the saints" (Jude 1:3). The faith that has already been delivered runs from Genesis to Revelation. There is a battle going on; a battle for the truth so we must strive to preserve what's already been delivered to the saints. We are not expecting any new deliveries because it was "once for all delivered."

Our fight for the faith makes us stronger in the faith. James wrote "For you know that the testing of your faith produces steadfastness" (James 1:3) so the testing of our faith, in fighting for the faith once delivered, produces a steadfastness for the Christian, so keep fighting the good fight of faith.

The very best possible fighting position that a believer could possibly take is on his or her knees because "The LORD will fight for you, and you have only to be silent" (Ex 14:14); in this way, God receives all the glory

Here are four very important Bible verses about fighting the good fight of faith. Offered by Jack Wellman, pastor of Heritage Evangelical Free Church in Udall, KS

1. 2 Timothy 4:7 "I have fought the good fight, I have finished the race, I have kept the faith."

The 2nd Book of Timothy and chapter four might be one of the most heart-breaking chapters for me to read. For one thing Paul wrote *"I am already being poured out as a drink offering, and the time of my departure has come. I have fought the good fight, I have finished the race, I have kept the faith"* (2 Tim 4:6-7) so he knew he was about to die and even though *"Demas, in love with this present world, has deserted me and gone to Thessalonica. Luke alone is with me"* (2 Tim 4:10-11a).

Paul wrote that *"At my first defense no one came to stand by me, but all deserted me. May it not be charged against them"* (2 Tim 4:16) so in the end, all had forsaken him but only *"the Lord stood by me and strengthened me, so that through me the message might be fully proclaimed and all the Gentiles might hear it. So I was rescued from the lion's mouth. The Lord will rescue me from every evil deed and bring me safely into his heavenly kingdom. To him be the glory forever and ever. Amen."* (2 Tim 4:17-18).

2. 1 Timothy 6:12 "Fight the good fight of the faith. Take hold of the eternal life to which you were called and about which you made the good confession in the presence of many witnesses."

This is one of the clearest commands in the Bible that we are to fight the good fight of the faith but what is this fight about? Paul specifies it's about the Christian faith and the battle ground for the fight is about preserving the faith just like Jude wrote, *"contend for the faith that was once for all delivered to the saints"* (Jude 1:3). The faith that has already been delivered runs from Genesis to Revelation. There is a battle going on; a battle for the truth so we must strive to preserve what's already been delivered to the saints. We are not expecting any new deliveries because it was "once for all delivered." I would say truth is worth fighting for.

3. Ephesians 6:12 "For we do not wrestle against flesh and blood, but against the rulers, against the authorities, against the cosmic powers over this present darkness, against the spiritual forces of evil in the heavenly places."

Jacob wrestled with God but he had been wrestling with a lot of others before this. His name means "supplanter" or "deceiver." After Jacob had wrestled with God, he realized that *"I have seen God face to face, and yet my life has been delivered"* (Gen 32:20). Jacob's name was later changed to Israel as God said *"you have striven with God and with men, and have prevailed"* (Gen 32:28).

Today, we wrestle against an unseen enemy. Satan and his demons are spirit beings but very powerful ones too and because of this, it is necessary to put on *"the whole armor of God, that you may be able to stand against the schemes of the devil"* (Eph 6:11).

4. James 1:12 "Blessed is the man who remains steadfast under trial, for when he has stood the test, he will receive the crown of life, which God has promised to those who love him."

How blessed is the man or woman who remains firm in their faith, remaining steadfast even under trial. Just as God told ancient Israel, He says to us *"You shall not fear them, for it is the LORD your God who fights for you"* (Deut. 3:22).

The things we fear the most like trials, financial difficulties, and relationship problems are best handled by letting God handle them. Commit it to prayer and then commit it to God because he alone can direct even a pagan king's heart (Prov 21:1) so don't be like *"those who shrink back and are destroyed, but of those who have faith and preserve their souls"* (Heb 10:39).

Fighting the good fight of faith is to…"Take hold of the eternal life to which you were called when you made your good confession in the presence of many witnesses" (1 Timothy 6:12, NIV)

We seek after it until we capture it and then we do not let it go. The thing we go after to capture is the gospel of Jesus Christ. This is where we discover salvation and the hope of eternal life and the fellowship of the Spirit and the grace of God. We are ever mindful of its power and blessings that befall those that are exercised by it.

We must stand firm in our faith, knowing that we are the children of God and have overcome them: because greater is he that is in you, than he that is in the world." John 4:4

The battle is the Lord's and we have the joy of ruling with him until all is finished and peace is restored in God's kingdom.

CHAPTER EIGHT:
THE BELIEVER'S AUTHORITY

If you are a "Born Again" believer, you have the Holy Spirit dwelling inside of you. "What? know ye not that your body is the temple of the Holy Ghost which is in you, which ye have of God, and ye are not your own?" I Corinthians 6:19

If the Holy Spirit really dwells in you, he is greater than anyone or any spirit, even Satan. "You are of God, little children, and have overcome them, because he who is in you is greater than he who is in the world. One greater than every demon, storm, trial, lack, attack, or depression is living in you today. He is more powerful than any sickness, disease, or affliction." I John 4:4 Are we in agreement so far?

If you are walking with the Lord, being filled with his Spirit, you have spiritual authority. Here are a few Bible references related to the believer's authority

Mark 16:17 ...And these signs will accompany those who believe: in my name they will cast out demons; they will speak in new tongues;

James 4:7 ...Submit yourselves therefore to God. Resist the devil, and he will flee from you.

Luke 10:19 ...Behold, I have given you authority to tread on serpents and scorpions, and over all the power of the enemy, and nothing shall hurt you.

Matthew 16:19 ...I will give you the keys of the kingdom of heaven, and whatever you bind on earth shall be bound in heaven, and whatever you loose on earth shall be loosed in heaven."

1 Peter 5:8 …Be sober-minded; be watchful. Your adversary the devil prowls around like a roaring lion, seeking someone to devour.

Luke 10:19-21 …Behold, I have given you authority to tread on serpents and scorpions, and over all the power of the enemy, and nothing shall hurt you. Nevertheless, do not rejoice in this, that the spirits are subject to you, but rejoice that your names are written in heaven. In that same hour he rejoiced in the Holy Spirit and said, "I thank you, Father, Lord of heaven and earth, that you have hidden these things from the wise and understanding and revealed them to little children; yes, Father, for such was your gracious will."

1 John 4:4 … Little children, you are from God and have overcome them, for he who is in you is greater than he who is in the world.

Revelation 12:11 …And they have conquered him by the blood of the Lamb and by the word of their testimony, for they loved not their lives even unto death.

Mark 11:23 …Truly, I say to you, whoever says to this mountain, 'Be taken up and thrown into the sea,' and does not doubt in his heart, but believes that what he says will come to pass, it will be done for him.

Hebrews 4:12 …For the word of God is living and active, sharper than any two-edged sword, piercing to the division of soul and of spirit, of joints and of marrow, and discerning the thoughts and intentions of the heart.

Acts 1:8 …But you will receive power when the Holy Spirit has come upon you, "and you will be my witnesses in Jerusalem and in all Judea and Samaria, and to the end of the earth."

John 14:12 …"Truly, truly, I say to you, whoever believes in me will also do the works that I do; and greater works than these will he do, because I am going to the Father."

Luke 10:17-19 …The seventy-two returned with joy, saying, "Lord, even the demons are subject to us in your name!" And he said to them, "I saw Satan fall like lightning from heaven. Behold, I have given you authority to tread on serpents and scorpions, and over all the power of the enemy, and nothing shall hurt you."

Mark 6:13 ...And they cast out many demons and anointed with oil many who were sick and healed them.

Ephesians 6:10-18 ...Finally, be strong in the Lord and in the strength of his might. Put on the whole armor of God, that you may be able to stand against the schemes of the devil. For we do not wrestle against flesh and blood, but against the rulers, against the authorities, against the cosmic powers over this present darkness, against the spiritual forces of evil in the heavenly places. Therefore take up the whole armor of God, that you may be able to withstand in the evil day, and having done all, to stand firm. Stand therefore, having fastened on the belt of truth, and having put on the breastplate of righteousness, ...

Matthew 28:18-20 ...And Jesus came and said to them, "All authority in heaven and on earth has been given to me. Go therefore and make disciples of all nations, baptizing them in the name of the Father and of the Son and of the Holy Spirit, teaching them to observe all that I have commanded you. And behold, I am with you always, to the end of the age."

Psalm 91:13 ...You will tread on the lion and the adder; the young lion and the serpent you will trample underfoot.

Acts 2:39 ...For the promise is for you and for your children and for all who are far off, everyone whom the Lord our God calls to himself.

Matthew 10:1 ...And he called to him his twelve disciples and gave them authority over unclean spirits, to cast them out, and to heal every disease and every affliction.

Acts 16:18 ...And this she kept doing for many days. Paul, having become greatly annoyed, turned and said to the spirit, "I command you in the name of Jesus Christ to come out of her." And it came out that very hour.

Acts 3:6 ...But Peter said, "I have no silver and gold, but what I do have I give to you. In the name of Jesus Christ of Nazareth, rise up and walk!"

Luke 10:1-42 ...After this the Lord appointed seventy-two others and sent them on ahead of him, two by two, into every town and place where he himself was about to go. And he said to them, "The harvest is plentiful, but the laborers are few. Therefore pray earnestly to the Lord of the harvest to send out laborers into his harvest. Go your way; behold, I am sending you out as lambs in the midst of wolves. Carry no moneybag, no knapsack, no sandals, and greet no one on the road. Whatever house you enter, first say, 'Peace be to this house!' ...

Acts 2:1-47 ...When the day of Pentecost arrived; they were all together in one place. And suddenly there came from heaven a sound like a mighty rushing wind, and it filled the entire house where they were sitting. And divided tongues as of fire appeared to them and rested on each one of them. And they were all filled with the Holy Spirit and began to speak in other tongues as the Spirit gave them utterance. Now there were dwelling in Jerusalem Jews, devout men from every nation under heaven. ...

Revelation 12:10 ... And I heard a loud voice in heaven, saying, "Now the salvation and the power and the kingdom of our God and the authority of his Christ have come, for the accuser of our brothers has been thrown down, who accuses them day and night before our God."

1 Corinthians 12:8 ...For to one is given through the Spirit the utterance of wisdom, and to another the utterance of knowledge according to the same Spirit,

We have the Spiritual authority or power of Jesus at our disposal. We can use it or not. If we don't, we will remain defeated and live in a carnal world being plagued by evil forces at every turn. It's far more to our advantage to stand up in the Lord and the power of his might and declare our freedom and walk in his Will.

As in most promises of God, it's up to us. God will not invade our free will. He will sit quietly by and watch us fall and then pick us up and start again to teach our hands to war so we can be victorious.

I Am A Believer & I Have Authority To
Spoil The Works of The Devil

When you believe, you rely upon, you adhere to and you trust in. That, my friends, is believing with the heart. That is what's necessary to overcome the rulers of darkness and win the battle. This is fighting the good fight of faith.

CONCLUSION

I hope tat this "Guide to Spiritual Warfare" has been helpful. Let us apply the scriptures to our daily experiences. We are encouraged by them to "Walk By Faith And Not By Sight." 2 Corinthians 5:7

The Bible says we are to fight the good fight. That suggests that there is also a bad fight. One can fight badly or outside of proper battle tactics. Hitler did that when he sent 29-million people to the gas chambers in WW II.

We want to use tactics that God has set up for us so we are assured of victory. If we run off in the flesh to fight a spiritual enemy, we will fail. That's doing things in bad form. It is not a good fight. The good fight of faith is a spiritual fight with spiritual weapons that have been provided by God for our use.

We must put on the entire armor of God and stand fast in the liberty Jesus gained for us on the cross. We must walk in the Spirit so we do not glorify the flesh. The deeds of the flesh will kill us over time. They tend to degrade our personalities, destroy our self-esteem and cause sadness, depression and guilt.

Remember, we do not fight with flesh and blood but rather with the rulers of darkness and spiritual wickedness in high places.

Jesus has already won this battle. All we need to do is stand fast, resist and take authority over all that is anti-Christ. If God is with us, who can be against us? No one that can win for we are already more than conquerors in Christ Jesus.

It's time to fight the good fight of faith

ABOUT THE AUTHOR
JOHN MARINELLI

Rev. Marinelli is an ordained minister, He has formed and been pastor of one church in Wisconsin and was the pastor of another in Alabama. He has also been a youth minister and evangelism director over the years.

Rev. Marinelli has authored several other books including: "Original Story Poems", "The Art of Writing Christian Poetry," "Pulpit Poems," "Moonlight & Mistletoe," "The Mysterious Stranger," "With Eagles Wings," "Mysteries & Miracles," "It Came To Pass," Why Do The Righteous Suffer," "Believer's Handbook of battle Strategies." "Hidden In Plain Sight" "The End of The World, From The Beginning, Shadows in the Light of a Pale Moon," "Mister Tugboat" "An Elephant Named Clyde" "Morning Reign" "Times Past But Not Forgotten" "How To Be Happy" and "How To Have A Victorious Christian Life."(www.marinellichristian-books.com)

John is an accomplished Christian poet. He also dabbles in songwriting, likes to play chess, sings karaoke and goes fishing now and then. He lives in north central Florida where he enjoys a retired lifestyle with his wife and two collies.

GALLERY OF ENCOURAGING CHRISTIAN POEMS

AGREEING WITH GOD

We speak of things that are not,
Believing in them as though they were,
Because our Heavenly Father spoke them first,
Sending them to us in promises that never blur.

We take Him at His Word,
And listen to all He has to say.
We wrap each promise around our souls,
Until what was spoken becomes our day.

We will agree with the Lord,
Trusting that He knows best.
For only His awesome power,
Can provide our souls with rest.

"As it is written, I have made thee a father of many nations, before Him who he believed, even God who quickens the dead and calls those things that be not as though they were" Romans 4:17

Like Abraham, we also have a destiny that God has spoken into our lives. He calls it forth before it exists. Like Abraham, we are to believe, even against hope, that what God said will indeed come to be. (Romans 4:18).

ARM'S LENGTH

I hold the world at arm's length,
That its choices do not interfere.
While it does its own thing,
I watch and wait over here.

My steps must not go that way,
For it's not where I need to be.
The Lord has shown me the path,
That will lead me to my destiny.

The call of the world is strong
And pulls at me now and then.
But I know that way
Is full of sorrow and sin.

I must move on in life
Beyond their beckoning call.
It's the right thing to do,
So I do not stumble or fall.

I will not be swayed or misled
By family, friends or business deal.
Their secret thoughts are not mine,
To consider, to admire or feel.

So I keep the world at "Arm's Length"
As I journey through this life.
My faith in Jesus keeps me strong,
As I walk in His glorious light.

"Love not the world, neither the things that are in the world. If any man loves the world, the love of the Father is not in him. For all that is in the world, the lust of the flesh, the lust of the eyes and the pride of life, is not of the Father, but of the world. And the world passes away and the lust thereof: But he that doeth the will of God abides forever. I John 2:15-17

It is more important to know God and to follow after Him, than to become entangled in life's lustful traps: for if we were to gain the whole world and lose our own soul, how terrible would that be?

DON'T WORRY

Don't worry about tomorrow.
You did that yesterday.
Go on with your life
And remember always to pray.

Ask and it shall be given to you,
But this great truth you already know.
Rejoice and be happy, why? Because…
Your harvest comes from what you sow.

I will say it again and even more,
Until it becomes very very clear.
Tomorrow will take care of itself,
But worry is another word for fear.

Now here's what I want you to do.
Trust in the Lord and be of good cheer.
Drop the worry from your vocabulary
And cast out that demon of fear.

Worry is the flipside of faith. If you are walking in faith, you are free from worry. Why, because faith hopes in God and trusts that he will be there to meet your need.

TWO HOUSES

We built our homes together,
Mine upon a Rock and his in the sand.
He thought his would be all right,
But he was a foolish man.

God's wisdom showed me the way.
And what I needed to do,
But my foolish neighbor,
Never had a clue.

Then the rains came,
And the winds began to blow.
The storms beat upon our homes,
And we had nowhere to go.

We built our homes together,
My neighbor and me.
Mine is still there upon the Rock,
But his ceased to be.

Wise men and fools both suffer,
The storms that befall mankind.
But those who trust in Jesus
Will always stand the test of time.

Foundation is everything. If you build your life on the Word of God, it will last forever. That's why we strive to be obedient to the will of God. We want his destine and his blessings, no matter what the world system thinks or does.

CLUTTER

Clutter keeps the mind confused,
As images dance through the night.
Lost among those unimportant thoughts,
Are the dreams that once shined bright.

An endless parade of fear and doubt,
Crowds the mind to destroy our day.
Ever soaring on the wings of the soul,
Until it has formed an evil array.

But clutter is by one's choice,
Of those who dance to its beat.
Better to face imaginations' due
Than to fall into utter defeat.

Be Quiet!!! Is our spirit's desperate cry,
As we call upon the name of the Lord.
Silence is our heart's desired prayer,
Until our minds are again restored.

"Keep thy heart with all diligence: for out of it are the issues of life" Proverbs 4:23

We make the final choices in life that either lead us astray or closer to the Lord. We chose what enters our hearts and fills our minds. May we always choose the path of righteousness and the way of peace.

THE LORD'S LITTLE

TWO BY FOUR

God has a little 2' X 4'
That rest on heaven's windowsill.
He uses it now and then,
When we stray from His will.

Sometimes we need a good "Bap";
With the Lord's little 2' X 4'
To knock out the confusion,
And help us to desire Him more.

The Lord's little 2' X 4'
Is what we sometimes need,
To get our thinking straight,
And keep our focus indeed.

The Lord's little 2' X 4'
Is fashioned from life's every trial,
So we do not stray from His will,
Or fall into an ungodly lifestyle.

"My son, despise not the chastening of the Lord; neither be weary of His correction: for whom the Lord loves, He corrects; even as a father his son, in whom he delights." Proverbs 3:11 & 12

It is a good thing to be corrected by God. We should not fear His rebuke for it is not His wrath, but rather a blessing from His love that keeps us moving on towards maturity.

I FIND MYSELF IN GOD

I find myself in God.
He is my, "Everything"
I know that He is Lord,
My Life, My Hope, My King.

I find myself in God,
Not the ways of Sin.
Nor do I look to others,
To know who I really am.

I find myself in God,
To whom I bow on bended knee.
He alone is my joy and strength
And where I want to be.

"For we are His workmanship, created in Christ Jesus unto good works, which God hath before ordained, that we should walk in them" Ephesians 2:10

Knowing that we are created in Christ Jesus gives us confidence to walk in Christ, as He walked, along a pathway of good works. It is our joy and pleasure to be like Him. In Him we move and live and have our being.

"I AM" THERE

"I AM" There,
At the end of your broken dreams,
Before the sun rises over your day,
Prior to those tear-filled streams.

"I AM" There,
Down that road of despair,
When all appears to be lost,
And no one seems to care.

"I AM" There,
Over all of life's twists and turns,
When tomorrow is all but gone,
And when you are full of concerns.

"I AM" There,
Sayeth the Lord of Host,
To bring you hope and peace,
And the power of My Holy Ghost.

"I AM" There,
To be sure you make it through,
In the midst of every trial,
To bless your life and deliver you.

"I Am" There

"All power is given unto me in heaven and earth. Go ye therefore and teach all nations, baptizing them in the name of the Father, and of the Son, and of the Holy Ghost: Teaching them to observe all things, whatsoever I have commanded you: and lo, I am with you always, even unto the end of the world." Mathew 28:18-20

The Lord is with us always. He never leaves our side, even when we leave His. In every situation, He is there. It's time to count on His presence and trust in His care.

SO LISTEN UP

I write this verse that all should know.
What I have to say is like a seed, ready to grow.
So listen up to all I have to say.
It could be the very blessing your heart needs today.

God has not given you a spirit of fear.
Instead, He has offered to dry up every tear.
He really loves you, even though you often fail.
His love and mercy follows you,
Enabling you to be the head and not the tail.
So do not worry or even fret.
That's why Jesus paid sin's awful debt.
Now go on in life to discover its victory
Knowing that Jesus has indeed set you free.

"For God hath not given us the spirit of fear: but of Power and of Love and a sound mine" II Timothy 1:7

There is nothing to fear except fear itself and that spirit has been defeated on the cross. We now have the Spirit of power and love and a sound mind. He will never leave us or forsake us. We are truly free.

WINNING THE BATTLE

We must use the Word of God
To calm emotions that fray.
For the enemy never sleeps,
Until he has led us astray.

So when your emotions overflow
With feelings like depression and fear.
Know this! If you dwell in that place,
You invite the enemy to draw near.

When your emotions rage
With fiery darts aglow,
Stand in the power of the Lord,
Against its awful woe.

And if you get confused
And lost in the storm,
Put your thoughts on trial,
Rejecting all but heaven born.

You can win the battle
That rages within your soul.
By casting down imaginations,
And breaking Satan's hold.

Remember to focus on Jesus,
Holding the world at arm's length.
Lift up your head above the trial,
And the Lord will give you strength.

"For the weapons of our warfare are not carnal but mighty, through God, to
the pulling down of strongholds: casting down imaginations and every high

thing that exalts itself against the knowledge of God, and bringing into captivity every thought to the obedience of Christ." II Corinthians 10:3-5 The battle is in our minds and we win by putting our thoughts on trial and casting out all that oppose the knowledge of God. This is true victory.

THE LIGHTHOUSE

A lighthouse is a blessing,
To the ships that toss in the sea.
For it shows them the way,
Until they can clearly see.

The rage of an angry storm,
Cannot hide its brilliant light.
Nor can its awesome furry,
Rule as an endless night.

Jesus is the lighthouse,
For those who have gone astray.
The light of His love,
Offers a new and living way.
Jesus is the lighthouse,
When fear and sickness rage.
The light of His love,
Gives hope in difficult days.

So trust in the Lord,
And look for His light.
He alone is "The Lighthouse",
That guides you through the night.

"I am the Way, the Truth, and the Life. No man cometh to the Father but by me" John 14:6

Life holds many dark nights that are full of unexpected storms. Only a deep abiding faith in Jesus Christ will get us through. He is the light of the world. His light keeps us from falling into confusion, sorrow, sickness and demonic oppression.

THE WAY MAKER

Only Jesus can make a way,
Through the difficulties of life.
He alone is Lord and King,
Over life's sorrows and strife.

He is the "Way Maker,"
When there is no visible way.
He will make the way known,
As though it were the light of day.

He will make a way,
For those of humble heart.
He will clear away the rubble,
Restoring what Satan broke apart.
Jesus is the "Way Maker,"
A friend to all who are lost.
He has made the way,
Paying sin's incredible cost.

The way to the Maker,
Is through His only Son.
He alone is the "Way Maker,"
Until life's battles are won.

"Let not your heart be troubled. Ye believe in God, believe also in me. In my father's house are many mansions: If it were not so, I would have told you. I go to prepare a place for you. And if I go and prepare a place for you, I will come again, and receive you unto myself, that where I am, there ye may be also." John 14: 1-3

The Lord is prepared for any emergency. He knows the beginning from the end and has gone before us to prepare a way that we can follow until we see Him face to face.

STINKING THINKING

Stinking thinking, they say,
Is bad for your health.
For it frustrates life's goals,
And denies happiness and wealth.

A right perspective is important,
As we think about everything.
It will either bring us down,
Or cause us to shout and sing.

What we think about these days,
Really does affect our life.
It can cause us to overflow with Joy,
Or fall into depression and strife.

So don't let your thinking,
Stink all the way up to heaven.
Stand in faith before God,
And get rid of that negative leaven.

"Then Jesus said unto them, take heed and beware of the leaven of the Pharisees and the Sadducees" Mathew 16:6

Someone once said, "We are what we think" The Bible says, "As a man thinks, so is he" It is important to concentrate our thinking of those things that are of good report, pure, honest and that will keep us clean of heart.

WISE MEN STILL SEEK HIM

Wise men still seek Him
Who appeared so long ago.
They come now by grace
Through faithful hearts aglow.

Wise men still seek Him
For He is their "Bread of Life."
A sustaining inner strength
Through times of sorrow or strife.

Wise men still seek Him
The Christ of Calvary.
God's only begotten Son
Crucified as Sin's penalty.

Wise men still seek Him
Jesus, God in human array.
King of kings & Lord of lords
Born to earth on Christmas Day.

"Now when Jesus was born in Bethlehem of Judea in the days of Herod the king, behold, there came wise men from the east to Jerusalem, saying, where is he that is born king of the Jews? For we have seen his star in the east and are come to worship him" Mathew 2:1-2

Seeking Jesus is the wisest thing any man, woman or child can do and when we find Him, it is our privilege to bow down and worship Him. This is our journey, our destiny and our life while on this earth.

THE ANGELS CRY HOLY

The Angels cry "Holy,"
While sorrow fills the land.
For God's Judgment Day,
Is to come upon every man.

The Angels cry "Holy,"
While mankind goes astray,
Rejecting the love of God,
To follow his own precarious way.

The Angels cry "Holy,"
Knowing the terror of the Lord,
When all who dwell in sin,
Will suddenly be destroyed.

The Angels cry "Holy,"
Waiting for all things new,
Born of the Holy Spirit,
When God's Judgment is through.

The Angels cry "Holy,"
"Holy is the Lamb,"
Waiting for the children of God,
To join "The Great I AM"

"And one cried unto another and said, "Holy, Holy, Holy, is the Lord of host: the whole earth is full of his glory" Isaiah 6:3

We serve a Holy God that deserves our reverence and homage. The angels know this and worship Him, but man, because of sin, has no real concept of his own creator.

A HIGHWAY CALLED "HOLINESS"

He places my feet on
A highway called "Holiness,"
That led my soul
To the throne of God.

Amidst the cheers of angels,
I walk, wearing His holy gown.
Onward towards heaven's throne,
While evil cast its awful frown.

My eyes were opened
That I might see.
Both the good and the evil,
That sought after me.

I walk the highway-Holiness
That crosses all of time.
Towards the throne of God,
Leaving this world behind.

"And an highway shall be there, and a way, and it shall be called, the way of holiness; the unclean shall not pass over it; but it shall be for those: the wayfaring men, though fools, shall not err therein. No lion shall be there, nor any ravenous beast shall go up thereon, it shall not be found there, but the redeemed shall walk there. And the redeemed of the Lord shall return, and come to Zion with songs and everlasting joy upon their heads: They shall obtain joy and gladness, and sorrow and sighing shall flee away. " Isaiah 35:8-10

What a privilege to walk the highway of Holiness. It is prepared especially for us, the redeemed, and it is protected from the errors of fools and the snarl of beast and especially the roar of the lion.

CALL UPON THE LORD

When your burdens overwhelm you,
Like a mighty raging sea.
Call upon the Lord, Jesus,
And He will set you free

When your heartaches are many,
And life is difficult to understand.
Call upon the Lord, Jesus.
He will come and hold your hand.

When your friends reject you,
Because you follow after Him,
Call upon the Lord, Jesus.
And keep yourself from sin.

When you fall into depression,
As though it were a giant pit.
Call upon the Lord, Jesus,
Who will restore your joyful wit.

When you're saddened by the day
Feeling lost and all alone.
Call upon the Lord, Jesus,
Who will make His way known.

When you are weary and heavy laden,
Tired from life's many tests.
Call upon the Lord, Jesus,
Who is sure to give you rest.

"Hear my cry; oh God, attend unto my prayer. From the end of the earth,

I will cry unto thee, when my heart is overwhelmed: Lead me to the rock that is higher than I." Psalms 61:1-2

Calling upon the Lord in stressful times is o.k. He wants us to cry to Him and then to trust in Him to watch over His Word to perform it on our behalf.

IT CAME TO PASS

Things often come to pass,
But seldom do they ever last.
They come into our busy day,
For awhile, then pass away.

We hear their voices, loud and clear,
As they arrive and while they are here.
They speak both joy and misery,
Some to you and some to me.

We say, "It came to pass,"
Or say, "It happened so fast."
Down life's beaten path,
Comes both love and wrath.

So say goodbye to sad and blue.
To all that is now troubling you.
For things will come, only to pass,
But God's love will always last.

"And it came to pass in those days…" Luke2:1

These are the times of our lives. We live them, some for good and some for not so good. One thing is for sure, that which comes our way, comes only to pass on by. It is not what happens that is so important, but rather what we do with what we are faced with.

Trusting in the Lord and seeking His guidance will always conquer that which comes to pass.

THE WHOSOEVER SCENARIO

The "Whosoever" is who so ever,
Not who so won't, can't or will not.
The story is as clear as a sunny day.
God offers a new and living way.

But only those who engage "free will"
To choose life, faith and obedience,
Will find salvation for their souls,
And be cleansed and made whole.

We do the choosing: to accept or deny.
That is how God set it up to be.
He made the call to life's "Whosoever",
That they could live abundantly.

"For God so loved the world, that he gave his only begotten son, that whosoever believeth in him, should not perish but have everlasting life." John 3:16

We are the "Whosoever" in John 3:16, that one day put his or her faith in Christ, believed in Him and now rest in the Lord's love and grace. We have the promise of God that He sent His Son so we could believe and have everlasting life. How great is that?

LITTLE PRISONS

Little prisons await the man with a lustful soul.
Bars of selfishness and pride create dungeons of icy cold.

Prisons of shame and jealousy fill the heart with utter despair.
Bars that separate from God and those that really care.

Stand back! While the doors are tightly closed;
Taking away your life, to wither as a dying rose.

Beware of those little prisons that trap the lustful soul.
Keep yourself free from sin through faith in the Christ of old.

Little prisons need not to be your fate.
It is your choice, Spirit or flesh to date.

"O Foolish Galatians, who hath bewitched you, that ye should not obey the truth, before whose eyes Jesus Christ hath been, evidently set forth, crucified among you? Are you so foolish? Having begun in the Spirit, are you now made perfect in the flesh?

We should always seek to dwell in the Spirit, that we would not emulate the deeds of the flesh. When we fall short, we create "little prisons" that keep us in confusion and away from the blessing of God. It's time to walk in the Spirit and break the prisons that so easily beset us.

REST MY CHILD

Rest my child, says the Lord.
Take thy peace and be restored.
I have provided, thy mouth to feed.
From the beginning, I knew your need.

Do not worry, fret or even fear,
For, my child, I am always near
To bless thy soul with love and grace,
To be with thee, face to face.

Come, my child, near to my throne.
Do not allow your faith to roam.
For those who will not believe
Can never find rest in times of need.

My Word shall see you through.
My grace I freely give to you
That you should rest, thy soul to keep,
Forever delivered from unbelief.

Resting in the Lord is the best way to stay happy. However, it requires faith and trust in God that he will be there for you when you need him. It's kind of neat to relax when fear and anxiety are knocking at your door.

A WHISPER IN THE WIND

There's a whisper in the wind
That lingers both day and night.
A champion of truth and justice,
By the power of His might.

A word in due season
That echoes from deep within.
A voice out of nowhere,
Reproving the world of sin.

Look there, in the street
And here, by the shores of the sea.
There's a whisper hidden in the wind;
A voice from eternity.

There's a calling from God.
His voice is hidden in the wind.
In a whisper, He speaks to our hearts
With the love and counsel of a friend.

Listen for the Whisper,
All who seek to know.
It is God's Holy Spirit
Telling you which way to go.

"And thine ears shall hear a word behind thee saying, This is the way, walk ye in it, when ye turn to the right hand and when ye turn to the left" Isaiah 30:21

The voice of the Lord is often a still small voice, yet always clear and it never brings confusion. His voice is like a whisper in the wind that brings a peaceful breeze to the heart. The joy of hearing His voice is to know His will and our destiny.

FRAGILE FLOWER RED

As a flower in earthen sod,
I bloom for thee, oh God.
To blossom with the turn of spring;
To be to you, a beautiful thing.

I lift my Fragile Flower Red
Upward from my earthen bed;
To draw light from God above,
Strength and peace and joy and love.

As a flower, I bloom for thee
That passersby may stop and see.
Your fragrance and beauty I am,
Flowered in grace as a man.

As a flower in earthen sod,
I bloom for thee, oh God.
Upward, I lift my head,
As a Fragile Flower Red.

"Be not conformed to this world, but be ye transformed, by the renewing of your mind, that ye may prove what is that good and acceptable and perfect will of God."

When we look to God as our source, we blossom, much like a flower that draws light from the sun. When we blossom, like a flower, we display the glory and beauty of our creator to all who care to stop and look. This is our divine destiny.

Other books by John Marinelli can be viewed and purchased at: www.marinellichristianbooks.com

Printed in May 2023
by Rotomail Italia S.p.A., Vignate (MI) - Italy